Nathan Lewis Rice

Lectures on Slavery

Delivered in the North Presbyterian Church, Chicago

Nathan Lewis Rice

Lectures on Slavery
Delivered in the North Presbyterian Church, Chicago

ISBN/EAN: 9783744732444

Printed in Europe, USA, Canada, Australia, Japan

Cover: Foto ©Lupo / pixelio.de

More available books at **www.hansebooks.com**

DELIVERED IN THE

NORTH PRESBYTERIAN CHURCH,

CHICAGO.

BY N. L. RICE, D.D.

CHICAGO:
DAILY DEMOCRAT PRINT, 45 LA SALLE ST.
1860.

LECTURE I.

IS SLAVEHOLDING SIN PER SE?

There are several reasons which have constrained me to depart from my usual course of pulpit instruction, and to enter upon a careful discussion of the subject of Slavery.

1. It has important bearings upon the question of the inspiration of the Scriptures. It is well known, that extreme views of both sides of this question have exhibited strong tendencies to infidelity. Extreme pro-slavery men are tempted to deny the Scripture doctrine of the unity of the human race; whilst not a few extreme anti-slavery men have fallen into fanatical infidelity. The correct statement and defence of the real teachings of the Scriptures on this subject, and of the legitimate tendencies of those teachings, will confirm their inspiration.

2. This subject has important bearings upon the unity, the peace, the honor and the efficiency of the Church of Christ. We are all familiar with the painful agitations and divisions which, during the last twenty years, have resulted from the different opinions entertained by ministers and laymen. The injury to the cause of religion and of sound morals, resulting from these agitations, is incalculable; and the end is not yet. There may be little reason to hope, in the present state of feeling, to accomplish much for the peace and unity of the Church by discussion; yet firmly believing, that the great body of good men would stand nearly together, if they understood each other, I feel constrained to make the effort to promote so desirable an end.

3. This subject has important bearings upon the Church of which I am an humble minister. It is almost the only Church, strong in the North and in the South, that, thus far, has withstood the divisive influences, and still resists the tendencies to both ex-

tremes.   Standing thus between two extreme parties, she has
had the fortune to be charged with holding precisely opposite
doctrines.   The extreme men of the South have labored to prove
that she holds to Abolitionist views ; whilst those at the North
are no less confident, that she is pro-slavery.   These opposite
charges, made by intelligent and even religious men, in view of
the same documents, do indeed give a sad exhibition of the
weakness of the human intellect, when under the influence of
strong prejudices.   But since it is impossible, that both these
opposite and contradictory charges can be true ; and since the
parties making them are equally prejudiced ; the strong proba-
bility, even before examination, is—that neither is true.   I need
scarcely say, that in this latitude constant efforts have been, and
still are made, to heap reproach upon the Presbyterian Church,
because of her supposed connection with slavery.   No one can
be ignorant of this fact, who has read either the religious or
political papers.   The time has fully come, then, for us clearly
to define our own position.   Presbyterians have never been
accustomed either to conceal their faith, or to shrink from the
defence of it.   It has not been characteristic of them to yield to
the winds of doctrine blowing around them, or to turn their backs,
when assailed.   It is especially proper for *me* to do this, inasmuch as the last paper adopted by the General Assembly on the
subject of slavery, and which has been endorsed by two succeeding Assemblies, was drafted by myself; and inasmuch as the last
Assembly, with extraordinary unanimity, honored me with a
Professorship in the important Theological Seminary founded in
this city.   On these accounts it is, doubtless, that the enemies of
the Church have, of late, directed their attacks specially against
me—hoping thereby to damage the Church.   It becomes especially my duty, therefore, to defend her against these assaults.

4. It has important bearings on our country.   The agitations of
which I have spoken, have not been confined to the churches.
For years past, they have produced increasing alienation between
the two great sections of the country.   This alienation has been
fearfully increased, of late, by the dreadful occurrences with which
we are painfully familiar.   The political parties, too, now stand
so arrayed against each other, as greatly to intensify this state
of feeling.   Heretofore, Americans have been accustomed to
rejoice in the certain progress and growing greatness of this highly
favored nation ; and have cherished the belief, that it was des-

tined, in the purposes of God, to have a mighty instrumentality in giving pure religion and religious liberty to the world. But now wise men and true patriots look with dread and alarm to the future, and their hearts are filled with forebodings of coming ruin. Surely the day has come, for those who can look calmly at the subject, to make some effort to save the heritage of our fathers, and to avert the horrible disasters that seem just before us.

The connection of the question of slavery with the politics of the country, renders the discussion of it more difficult, and yet the more necessary. Let us try to lose sight of political parties, whilst we calmly seek for light from the word of God.

As to *myself*, I have not the slightest interest in slavery. I never owned a slave, and do not expect to. I have resided and labored in both the slave-holding and the free States. I have seen slavery as it is, and have been intimately acquainted with many slave-holders. I have made the subject one of careful study more than thirty years, and have watched the workings of the different modes of dealing with it. It may be supposed, there-fore, that my opinions are definitely formed. If I know myself at all, my earnest desire is to see every human being as free as I am; and to effect such an object, I would exert myself as earnestly, on any feasible plan, as any living man.

The discussion of slavery presents a moral phenomenon which, I believe, has not a parallel in the history of moral and religious investigations. The Church of God has had to deal with it nearly four thousand years, and through the whole of that period wise and good men have been, with comparatively few exceptions, very nearly agreed. And yet, during the last thirty or forty years, the constant, earnest discussion of it has resulted in no approximation to agreement, but in greater divergence. This is true, not only as between men in the free and slave-holding States, but as between men in the free States, and even in other countries. The divisions in churches, where formerly peace and unity existed, are the sad proof.

This state of things is the more remarkable, when we remem-ber, that the differences are not slight, but as between the darkness of midnight and the clear light of noonday. For example, Rev. James Duncan, in a book republished in 1840, by the Cincinnati Anti-Slavery Society, uses such language as this: "The crime of slave-holding may, by a very short process of reasoning, be shown to be much more aggravated than a common act of murder"—"a degree of theft as much more aggravated than horse-stealing, as a man is better than a horse." And a Congregational Association in the Northwest recently resolved, that "the practice of slaveholding is justly regarded as 'the sum of all villainies,'" and therefore, they refuse to hold Christian fellowship with slaveholders.

On the other hand, the General Assembly of the Presbyterian Church has decided that slave-holding is not, *in itself* a bar to Christian fellowship; and this ground has been occupied by such men as Rev. Dr. A. Alexander, and Dr. Hodge, of Princeton, Rev. Dr. Tyler, of East Windsor Theological Seminary, Drs. Cunningham and Chalmers, of Scotland, and a multitude of others, whose eminent learning and piety cannot be questioned. Dr. Chalmers pronounced the leading principle of Abolitionism, "a factitious and new principle, which not only wants, but which contravenes the authority of Scripture and Apostolic example, and, indeed, has only been heard of in Christendom within these few years, as if gotten up for an occasion, instead of being drawn from the repositories of that truth which is immutable and eternal." And the paper adopted by the General Assembly, already mentioned, which was denounced as making our Church, *par excellence*, the slave Church of America, called forth the unqualified admiration of Dr. Chalmers, who yet thought himself an enemy of slavery.

How shall we account for these radical differences on a great moral question, between men who profess to derive their principles from the same unerring rule? They may be accounted for, in part, from the fact, that too many Christian men derive their views of human rights from other sources, and then seek to justify them by appeals to the Scriptures. They are caused partly by widely different notions of men respecting what slavery is. They discuss the merits of different things under a common name, and thus reach opposite conclusions. And then the subject, as all who have attempted to investigate it know, is one of the most complicated in the whole range of moral questions. However the differences may be accounted for, the fact that men of learning and piety differ so widely, constitutes a very cogent reason, why no one should form an opinion without thorough examination. Declamation and denunciation on such a subject, are madness. If ever there was a subject which demanded careful, thorough, impartial examination, this does.

Some *five* different opinions are entertained respecting slavery. 1. That slaveholding is, like blasphemy, sin *per se*—always and in all circumstances sinful. 2. That although there may be cases in which the legal relation is justifiable, yet since slaveholders are generally tyrants and sinners, the fact that a man is a slaveholder, is *prima facie* evidence of sin; and it is for him to prove his innocence. This opinion reverses the legal principle, that a man is presumed to be innocent, till proved guilty. 3. That slavery is a great evil, originating in sin, but that circumstances may exist which justify slaveholding, for the time being. 4. That it is a purely civil matter, with which the Church has nothing to do, but to teach and enjoin the relative duties of master and slave. 5. That slavery is a Divine institution, or, at least, is *sanctioned* by the Bible.

Before we can hope to get a clear view of the moral character of slavery and slaveholding, we must obtain a distinct idea of what it is. On this subject more than on almost any other, men constantly confound the thing with the laws by which it is regulated. Let us try to get a satisfactory view of what slavery is in itself.

Some insist upon Aristotle's definition—"A slave is a tool with a soul in it." "Slavery," says a late writer of some notoriety, "is a system which divests human beings of the character and rights of persons, and reduces them to the character of *things* having no rights." If this is slavery, then I admit that slaveholding is always and everywhere a great sin, which ought to exclude from the Church of God. It requires no proof that that which robs a man of all rights, and makes him a *thing*, is sinful.

Professor Haven defines, or rather describes it thus: "When the right of personal ownership and personal control, that properly belong to a man, are taken from him, for no fault and by no consent of his own, and vested in another, giving to the latter control over the person and industry of the former, the man thus subjected becomes a slave, and the one to whom he is subjected is termed a master. * * * The ownership is complete, and, to a great extent, irresponsible. The slave is in the same category with any other property or possession—as truly the property of the master as the horses or dogs that belong to the same plantation. The control of the master over the one is as complete, unlimited, and irresponsible, as his control over the other. His time, his labor, his acquisitions, his person, his children, are not his own, but his master's. He is to be bought, and sold, and worked, and whipped, at the master's pleasure. He has *no rights of his own.*"

If this is a correct definition of slavery, I agree with Prof. Haven, that " it can hardly admit of serious question that slavery, as thus defined, involves a moral wrong"—that it is " contrary to the fundamental principles of morality." But his own statements, which are absolutely contradictory, are the best proof that it is not correct. In telling what a slave is, he informs us, that the control of the master over him is as complete, unlimited and irresponsible, as his control over his horses or dogs. And yet he admits, that limitations of his power may and do exist. And he also admits, " that slavery is *recognized* in the Scriptures both of the O. & N. Testament;" that " under the Jewish economy, slavery, in a modified form, existed, and was suffered to exist;" that " the power of the Jewish master over his servant was closely and strictly limited;" that " the servant was not, in the modern sense, a slave—a mere piece of property, a thing. He was still a man. He had *rights*, and they were carefully guarded and secured by law. The master was not, either in theory, or practically, irresponsible. In purchasing a servant, he purchased not so much the man himself, as the right to the labor and services of the man, and even that under certain important restrictions. * * * Religious rights were especially guaranteed to the servant," &c. Yet the Professor admits, that the man whose rights were thus guarded, was really a *slave.* He, therefore, admits that slavery does not necessarily give the master unlimited and irresponsible power, does not necessarily deprive the slave of all rights, and make him a *thing.* For if there has been a slavery, which recognized the slave as a man, and protected his rights as a man, there may be such slavery again. Nay—all that would be necessary to make the slavery of South Carolina just such, would be a modification of the laws regulating it, which Christianty may effect. And even without any change in the laws, Christian men may acknowledge and protect the rights of their slaves, as they did in the Apostolic age, under the code of Rome.

We are not now inquiring respecting either *modern* slavery or *ancient* slavery. We desire to ascertain what slavery is *in its essential nature ;* and then we can easily judge of the character of those laws which, though not essential to it, are often connected with it. We desire to know precisely what it is, because if the relation of master and slave is in itself sinful ; then a good man cannot be a slaveholder, even under God's law. Nay—on this supposition, God's law could not recognize it, and prescribe duties as growing out of it. If it is not, a good man may possibly be a slaveholder under a very bad civil code, governing his conduct by the Divine law. It is amazing that Prof. Haven should assert, that slavery is "contrary to the fundamental principles of morality," and yet that "it is recognized in the Scriptures, both of the O. & N. Testament," and " that it is not expressly and directly condemned or prohibited in either;" that such slavery as that of Rome was "tolerated" in the church by the Apostles ! How could they tolerate in the church a relation which reduced men to mere *tools*, depriving them of all rights, and which was in violation of the fundamental principles of morality ?

Paley defines slavery to be " an obligation to labor for the benefit of the master, without contract or consent of the servant." This definition was accepted by Dr. Wayland in his discussion with Dr. Fuller. According to Paley, this obligation may arise from *crime, captivity* or *debt*. This definition makes slavery a thing radically different from the first and second definitions given. It is, however, defective, in that it omits the corresponding obligations of the master.

The Princeton *Review* defines slavery to be the master's right to the service of the slave, involving the corresponding obligation to treat him as a *man*, guarding his rights as to family, compensation and religious instruction. *See Review Oct.* 1844.

I accept this definition. That it is the true one, will appear from a few considerations. And here it is important to remark, *that nothing should be allowed to enter into a definition, which does not necessarily belong to the thing defined.* To admit into a definition that which is merely accidental, or which may be absent, while yet the thing exists, is to confuse and mislead.

Bancroft says, in the Roman code of slavery, "no protection was afforded to limb or life." But in the slaveholding States in this country, the killing of a slave is *murder*. In Massachusetts colony it was enacted, "that all slaves shall have the liberties and Christian usage which the law of God, established in Israel concerning such persons, doth morally require." In Connecticut, not only was the killing of a slave murder, but the master was

liable to be sued by the slave "for beating, or wounding, or
for immoderate chastisement." A slave was also capable "of
holding property in character of a devisee or legatee.'—*Judge
Reeve.* According to the same authority, a slave in Connecticut,
differed from an apprentice mainly in that he served during life.
Dr. Thompson, of New York, an extreme Abolitionist, says,
"The Hebrew law of servitude regarded the slave as a *person*
under limited obligations to his master."

Now, since it is admitted that slavery has existed in different
countries, whilst the laws regulating it have differed very widely,
it is absurd to confound the thing itself with those laws which
may be repealed or changed without destroying it. Still more
absurd is it to judge of the character of Christian slaveholders
by the slave code of the State where they reside.

A broad distinction ought to be made between any system of
slavery, and slaveholding under or in connection with that system.
"Distinction," says Dr. Chalmers, "ought to be made between
the character of a system and the character of the persons whom
circumstances have implicated therewith." Let me try to make
this point clear.

Marriage is a divine institution, controled by Divine law, yet
recognized and, to some extent, controled also by civil law. The
civil laws which regulate it in any particular country, may be
very defective and even iniquitous; yet every good man, when
he enters into this relation, governs his conduct, not by the civil
law, but by the Divine law. The civil code of Rome, for example, gave the husband unlimited power over his wife, even to the
taking of her life; but no good man would do all that the civil law
permitted. The same may be said of the parental relation. Yet
under the worst laws there have been as kind husbands and
fathers, as under the best; because the law of God was their
rule of action. Slavery is a human, not a Divine institution,
controled by human law, yet recognized, though not *sanctioned*,
by the Scriptures, and regulated also by Divine law. None can
deny, that the Scriptures prescribe the relative duties of masters
and servants. Now, is it not perfectly clear, that a man who is
a husband, a father and a master, may as conscientiously obey
the Divine law in the last relation, as in the two former—even
though the civil code regulating it may be either defective or
most unrighteous? And is it not equally clear, that the civil
law may vary in its provisions from the iniquitous code of Rome

to the life-apprenticeship of Connecticut, without destroying the thing—slavery?

Holding, then, that slavery is nothing more than the claim of the master to the services of the slave, involving the obligation on the master's part to treat him as a *man*, and according to the directions of God's word, I propose to discuss three questions:

1. Is slaveholding, as thus defined, sinful in itself, as is blasphemy, to be abandoned instantly, without regard to circumstances? Or have circumstances existed, which, for the time, justified persons in holding slaves?

2. Do circumstances now exist, which, for the time, so justify persons in our country in holding slaves, that they may be properly recognized as Christians, in good standing in the Church of Christ?

3. What is the Scriptural and true method of dealing with slavery, as it exists in our country, so as most effectually to mitigate its evils whilst it continues, and most safely and speedily to abolish it?

In the discussion of this subject we meet with serious difficulties, arising from its very complicated character. We have to consider the relation itself of master and slave, whether it is essentially immoral—divested of all that is not essential to it. Then we have to consider Jewish slavery, Roman Slavery, American slavery. And in considering the last, there is a question respecting the duty of the States in which it exists. Is it their duty, as accountable to God for their legislation, immediately to abolish it? If not, is it their duty to adopt, at once, plans of gradual emancipation? Is it their duty to emancipate the slaves without colonization—leaving the whites and blacks together? Then arises the question, what is the duty of individuals and families, where slavery exists by law? Is it their duty immediately to emancipate their slaves? What is their duty as citizens, having a moral influence and a voice in the legislation of the country? Then there is a question respecting the duty of the churches in the slave States, and the duty of the Church, embracing the free and the slave States. It is extremely difficult, in the discussion of a subject so very complicated, to keep the several questions involved so separate, as to discuss them satisfactorily; and the difficulty is increased by the extent to which both moralists and popular writers and speakers have confounded them. Let me state very clearly my position.

1. I hold to *the unity* of the human race—that "God hath made of one blood all nations of men for to dwell on all the face of the earth."

2. Consequently I hold, that the command—"Thou shalt love thy neighbor as thyself"—applies, in its full force, to every human being. The golden rule—"Whatsoever ye would that men should do to you, do ye even the same unto them"—applies as fully to the Africans as to any other people. The curse pronounced upon Ham does not justify us in enslaving his descendants. I would not buy or hold a man as a slave, unless the circumstances were such, that I would justify him in buying and holding me, if our relative positions were changed. I would no sooner maltreat a slave or wound his feelings, than I would do the same thing to his master.

3. I do not hold, therefore, that slavery is a Divine institution, as is marriage, or the parental relation, or as is civil government; nor do I hold that the Bible *sanctions* slavery. To make the broad statement—that it sanctions slavery—would be to say, that it authorizes the strong to 'enslave the weak, whenever they are so disposed; and it might be construed to justify the abominable slave trade.

4. I distinctly deny the right of any man to traffic in human beings for gain, whether that traffic be the foreign or domestic slave trade. Men who engage in this inhuman business, are monsters.

5. I deny the right of any man to separate husbands and wives, parents and children, for his convenience, or for gain. The marriage of slaves, whether recognized by the civil law or not, is as valid in God's law, as that of their masters; and what "God has joined together, let not man put asunder."

6. I deny the right of any man to withhold from his slaves a fair compensation for their labor. Every master, remembering that his Master is in Heaven, with whom there is no "respect of persons," is bound to give them that which is "just and equal," taking into account, of course, his obligation to provide for them for life. What the services of any slave are worth, depends, as in the case of other men, on circumstances.

7. I hold it to be the duty of masters not only to give their slaves all needed food, clothing and shelter, and to treat them kindly, but to afford them the opportunity to receive religious instruction, and to read the word of God. Christ said—"Search

would refuse to be governed in the treatment of their slaves by
the law of God, instead of the existing civil code.

I must say, before proceeding with the argument, that I make
a distinction between the responsibility of those who *introduced*
slavery, and of those who *inherited* it. On this point I have
something to say hereafter. I only remark now—that one generation may introduce evils into a country, which it may require
several generations to remove.

Taking this view of the matter, I deny that the relation between
master and slave is *necessarily sinful*. In my debate with Rev.
Mr. Blanchard (as the representative of Gov. Chase and nine
other gentlemen) the following was the question : "*Is slaveholding
in itself sinful, and the relation between master and slave necessarily a sinful relation ?*" I then maintained, and now maintain,
the negative of this question, and proceed to the proof.

1. The first argument I offer, is a *presumptive* proof, viz: that the
overwhelming majority of wise and good men, in past ages and
in the present, have understood the Scriptures to teach that the
relation is not necessarily sinful. Dr. Chalmers, as already
remarked, pronounces the doctrine that slaveholding *is sin in
itself*, "a factitious and new principle, which not only wants, but
which contravenes the authority of Scripture and Apostolic
example, and, indeed, has only been heard of in Christendom
within these few years." Is it credible, that on such a subject,
the Church of God and all good men have been blind, utterly
misunderstanding the Scriptures, for eighteen hundred years ?
If so, we certainly need an infallible interpreter. It is a fact that
slavery existed in New England for many years, and was never,
to any extent, made a matter of discipline in the Churches at all,
till abolished by the civil law. This fact I stated on the floor of
the Consociation of Rhode Island, and it was not disputed.

It is moreover, a fact, stated by President Allen, and not
denied, that President Edwards, of whom the Congregationalists
of New England have been justly proud, lived and died a slaveholder, and after his death, his slave Titus was appraised at
thirty pounds. Many other good men, as the same authority
states, were slave-holders in New England. Beyond a doubt,
they believed themselves justified by the circumstances surrounding them. Moreover, the harmonious correspondence between
the Congretional bodies and our General Assembly, interrupted

only within a few years past, proves that they did not believe the Abolitionist doctrine. Nay, many of the first ministers in New England do not yet believe it; and the same may be said of eminent men in other denominations.

Is it credible that it could have been so difficult for the great body of good men to see this doctrine, if it had been clearly taught in the Bible?

2. My second proof that the relation of master and slave is not necessarily a sinful relation, is derived from the application of the *moral law* and the *golden rule* to the facts of the case. The principle of that law requires me, as far as other paramount duties permit, to improve the condition of my suffering fellow-men.

Now, it is a fact, admitted and asserted by Abolitionists, that the Roman slave code gave to the master unlimited power over the slave, even to the taking of his life. It is admitted, that the slaves of heathen masters were constantly exposed to the most cruel treatment, and even to be murdered for the most trivial offence, or for no offence. It is unquestionably true, that the Apostles and primitive Christians would have rejoiced to see that cruel code abolished, and to see the slaves enjoying freedom. But they could not purchase and emancipate them; but they might purchase and hold many of them as their own servants, or they might continue to hold those they possessed before their conversion. Now let us take our stand in one of those churches, addressed in the Epistles of Paul, and arraign the slaveholders amongst them. What is your charge against them? That they *reduced* those persons to slavery? No—for they found them slaves. That by purchasing or holding them they endorsed and upheld the infamous slave code of Rome? By no possible construction of their acts can you make out such a charge. That they have made the condition of the slave less tolerable than it was? This no one will pretend. What, then, is your charge? It must be—that they have greatly improved their condition, rendering it incomparably happier than it would have been! Do you call this a violation of the Divine law? Do you pronounce it inconsistent with "the golden rule?" Can you deny that the principles of true benevolence might and did require primitive Christians to hold slaves, who otherwise would have been in the hands of heathen masters?

That the Apostles did not approve of the Roman system of

slavery, is clear enough. That that system was utterly inconsistent with the principles of the Gospel, is equally clear. And
yet, though the Apostles could neither abolish nor modify the
laws respecting it, they evidently did justify christian men in
holding slaves, whose condition was far better in their hands,
than it could otherwise have been? And will any one deny, that
Christians in the slaveholding States may do the same thing for
the same reason? I have known instances in which slaves, in
the hands of cruel men, have been purchased by humane men,
at their own earnest and importunate request; and I have seen
their joy, when they passed out of the hands of such men.

Now, observe—the abolitionists take extreme ground—that
slaveholding is, in all cases, sinful. If, then, I can prove—that
any cases—especially great numbers of them—have existed, in
which, on the strictest interpretation of the word of God, the relation was not sinful; I have completely refuted their doctrine.
Perhaps the existence of slavery and the exposed condition of
the slaves, may explain the reason why Moses, under Divine
direction, allowed the Jews to hold slaves; and why the Apostles allowed Christians to do the same thing. The condition of
the slaves was far better in the hands of good men. This view
is surely far more honoring to Moses and the Apostles, and to
Christ, under whose guidance they acted, than that so commonly
urged by abolitionists, viz: that it was tolerated by Moses, as
"polygamy and similar kindred vices"—(Prof. Haven)—and that
the Apostles did not dare to attack the iniquity, lest they should
excite persecution! One cannot help feeling shocked at the
intimation, that God gave express permission to the Jews to
indulge in "polygamy and similar kindred vices;" and at the
intimation, that the Apostles admitted into the church men living
in a relation which was in violation of "the fundamental principles of morality." This leads to—

3. My third proof that the relation between master and slave
is not necessarily sinful, which is derived from the teaching and
the example of Christ and his Apostles. It is admitted, as we
have seen, that slavery existed and was recognized by the law
of Moses, amongst the Jews. Dr. Thompson, already quoted,
says,—"The ranks of slaves were recruited from thieves, debtors,
and captives in wars; but the slave was always treated as a
person; the laws were altogether in his favor; and *perpetual,
unmitigated chattleism was a thing unknown among the He-*

brews" I admit that *unmitigated chattleism* did not exist under the law of Moses, and that slaves were regarded as *persons*. Still Dr. T. admits that they were *slaves ;* and his own assertion that they were treated as persons, proves that real slavery may exist without unmitigated chattleism, and without reducing the slave to a *thing*. He says, further, " The enslaving of the heathen was permitted to the Israelites under certain regulations." Very good. But were they permitted to do a wicked thing, and to form a sinful relation, "under certain regulations?" Will this be pretended? If not, then slaveholding was not, in those circumstances, sinful.

In admitting, that the Jews were allowed to buy and hold slaves, Dr. Thompson has made no undue concession ; for the following language admits of no other construction : " Both thy bondmen and thy bondmaids, which thou shalt have, shall be of the heathen that are round about you; of them shall you buy bondmen and bondmaids. Moreover, of the children of the strangers, that do sojourn among you, of them shall you buy, and of their families that are with you, which they begat in your land ; and they shall be your possession. And you shall take them as an inheritance for your children after you, to inherit them for a possession ; they shall be your bondmen forever; but over your brethren of the Children of Israel, ye shall not rule one over another with rigor." *Levt.* 25:44,46.

It is admitted, likewise, that the Apostles did receive slave-holders into the churches, without requiring them to emancipate their slaves. On this point all commentators and critics, of any note, are perfectly agreed. I have already noticed the reference of Dr. Chalmers to " *Scripture and apostolic example,*" to prove Abolitionists in error. Mr. Barnes, of Philadelphia, who has published a book against slavery, says : " It is evident from this that there were in the Christian Church those who were *masters*, and the most obvious interpretation is that they were the owners of slaves. Some such persons would be converted, as such are now. Paul did not say that they could not be Christians. He did not say that they should be excluded at once from the communion. He did not hold them up to reproach, or use harsh and severe language toward them. He taught them their duty toward those who were under them, and laid down principles which, if followed, would lead ultimately to universal freedom. (*Comment on Eph.* 6.) Dr. Wayland, considered an Abolitionist,

B

says: " The moral *principles* of the Gospel are directly subversive of the principles of slavery; but, on the other hand, the Gospel neither *commands* masters to manumit their slaves, *nor authorizes* slaves to free themselves from their masters; and, also, it goes further, and *prescribes* the duties suited to both parties in their present condition." (*Mor. Philos. p.* 212.)

Dr. Tyler, of East Windsor Theological Seminary, said : " The simple question before us is this : Is slaveholding a sin, calling for the discipline of the Church ? And this is answered by the example of the Apostles. They lived and labored in the midst of it, and did not pronounce it a sin; and we may not and cannot do it."

Dr. Thompson himself, though so extreme an Abolitionist, says: " Hence the relation of master and servant was at once lifted (by the Apostles) out of the plane of the civil law into the higher plane of Christian love. The outward relation constituted by law might not cease, it might not be possible legally to terminate this, but the essence of slavery was abolished by the fundamental law of Christianity." This fundamental law, as stated by him, says: "All ye are *brethren;*" but he forgets that this applies only to *converted* slaves. And so far as they are concerned, Paul guards against the very conclusion to which Dr. T. comes, by commanding such servants to serve their " *believing masters*" (who were masters still) the more faithfully. 1 Tim. 6:1,2. " This shows," says Scott, the learned Commentator, " that Christian masters were not required to set their slaves at liberty; though they were instructed how to behave towards them in such a manner as would greatly lessen and nearly annihilate the evils of slavery."

Let us admit, however, all that Dr. T. has said. And now, if the relation of master and slave was necessarily sinful, or sinful in the circumstances, how could that relation be lifted up into the kingdom of Christ. Surely the Gospel could not thus lift up a sinful thing. But we do cheerfully admit, that the relation, *because it was not sinful, was* lifted up to a higher plane, whilst the legal relation continued ; and if unmitigated chattleism is the essence of slavery, certainly that was abolished. And so the Presbyterian church forbids masters to do many things which the civil law allows, and enjoins duties the civil law does not enforce. Thus she has lifted the relation to a higher plane.

Now, did the Apostles admit into the church, as Christian

brethren, men living in gross sin, without requiring them to abandon it? Did they so dishonor Christ, deceive sinful men, and corrupt the church?

It is surely remarkable that the man among the Jews who exhibited the greatest faith, was a Roman Centurion, who was a slaveholder. Whilst our Lord was at Capernaum, "a certain Centurion's servant, who was dear unto him, was sick, and ready to die." He called on Jesus to heal his servant, and the elders of the Jews said that he was worthy—"For he loveth our nation, and he hath built us a synagogue." The servant was healed; and Jesus said to the people: "I have not found so great faith, no not in Israel." This Centurion, Dr. Thompson admits, was a slaveholder; and we here see evidence that true affection can exist between a master and his slave. Our Lord healed the servant, but did not command the master to manumit him.

Strangely enough, Abolitionists quote Gal. 3:27, 28, in favor of their doctrine: "For as many of you as have been baptized unto Christ have put on Christ. There is neither Jew nor Greek, there is neither bond nor free, there is neither male nor female; for ye are all one in Christ. But is it true, that the Jew ceased to be a Jew, or a Greek ceased to be a Greek, when converted to Christianity? Will you say, *literally*, there is neither *male* nor *female*? This would leave the world in a somewhat anomalous and rather unpromising case. What does the passage mean? Why, simply, that as all men are equally sinners, so Christianity places all upon the same platform, *as sinners saved by grace*. But though the king and his meanest subject, as converted sinners, stand side by side; the king is still a king, and the subject still a subject. It is not true that the Gospel annihilates the distinctions in society. Strange how, in the effort to sustain a favorite doctrine, good men lose sight of the plainest principles of language.

On this passage Doddridge says—"Slaves are now the Lord's freemen, and freemen the Lord's servants; and this consideration makes the free humble, and the slave cheerful."

But the most amazing of all the statements we have seen, in the attempt to evade the force of a clear argument, is that of Dr. Thompson, in relation to "The Domestic Code of Rome." He tells us, the father had unlimited power over his children, and the husband unlimited power over the wife. Yet the New Testament is entirely silent with respect to this bloody code of domestic law. "Nowhere in that book can you find a command, 'Husbands, do not whip or kill your wives;' nowhere can you find a command, 'Fathers do not scourge your sons, nor sell or torture them, nor send them into exile, nor put them to death.'" But we do find such a command as this: "Husbands, love your wives, even as Christ loved the Church. So ought men to love their wives, as their own bodies. He that loveth his wife, loveth himself. For no man ever yet hated his own flesh, but nourisheth and cherisheth it, even as the Lord the Church." Can a man love his wife as Christ loved the Church, and yet whip or kill her? If not, then the New Testament does forbid such cruelty in the strongest possible manner. We do find such a command as this: "And ye fathers, provoke not your children to wrath; but bring them up in the nurture and admonition of the Lord." Can a father do this, and yet abuse or murder his son? If not, then the New Testament does, in the stoangest manner, forbid such cruelty. Strange, that in the vain effort to sustain Abolitionism, a minister of Christ would assert that the New Testament is silent respecting the cruel domestic code of Rome.

If all he means to prove by these extraordinary statements, was merely—that the Apostles never sanctioned the slave code of Rome; we cheerfully admit it. Most assuredly they never sanctioned that horrible code. But the question is, whether, notwithstanding that code, they did receive slaveholders into their churches, requiring them to govern their conduct by the Divine law; and if they did so, did they thus permit them to live in sin; or did the circumstances justify them, for the time, in holding slaves?

But it is admitted, the Apostles did receive slaveholders into the church, as faithful Christians; did they receive men guilty of abusing or murdering their wives and children? If they had done so, the case would have been a parallel one.

But it is said, though slaveholders were not commanded to manumit their slaves, the *principles* inculcated by the Apostles are subversive of slavery, and prove slaveholding sinful. I admit that the tendency of the Gospel is to remove all evils, and slavery amongst them. But suppose the Apostles had received thieves, liars, and drunkards into the church, without requiring them at once to abandon their evil practices, and had contented themselves with inculcating *principles*, which, if regarded, would ultimately remove such vices from the church, what would we say? But why not, if slaveholding is on a par with such sins?

If slaveholding was a sin, in the circumstances, it is certain that the Saviour and his Apostles treated it with a leniency which they showed to no other class of sins, and which they could not consistently show to any sin.

I have deemed it unnecessary to go fully into the argument to prove the facts, that the law of Moses permitted the Jews to purchase and hold slaves, and that slaveholders were received into the Apostolic churches ; because, as I have shown, leading Abolitionists admit them; and none can deny, that all commentators and expounders of the Bible, of any note, assert them.

I do not desire to draw any conclusions from this argument, which are not fully warranted. I do not profess to have proved, that slaveholding, *as it exists in this country*, is right or justifiable ; much less, that the slave codes of the South are right ; but I think I have clearly proved, both from the principles of the moral law, and from the teaching and example of Moses, of Christ and the Apostles, that the relation of master and slave *is not necessarily or always sinful;* that good men have been slaveholders ; that *circumstances have existed* which justified them, for the time being, in holding slaves.

Since, then, the rightfulness or sinfulness of slaveholding depends on *circumstances*, we cannot determine, in the case of any class of slaveholders, whether they are justifiable in holding slaves, until we have carefully examined the *circumstances* surrounding them. Consequently all wholesale condemnation of slaveholding is utterly unwarrantable.

I propose, on next Sabbath evening, to go into a careful examination of slavery, as it exists in this country, and to inquire, in the light of God's Word, how far Christians in the slaveholding States are justifiable in holding slaves ; and whether the Church can, on Scripture principles, refuse to hold fellowship with them.

Let me say, in conclusion, I think I can see how it is that so many Abolitionists have become infidels. They have gone aback of the Scriptures for their ideas of human rights. They have then exhausted their learning and skill in hair-splitting criticism upon the language of Inspiration, to compel it to utter the sentiments they have imbibed from other sources, until, vexed at the difficulties that press upon them, they have hurled the Bible from them, and resolved to walk in their own light.

You know, my friends, that I might gain popularity by falling in with the current that has set in so strongly in this latitude, and raising the Abolitionist shout. But I see before me an august tribunal, which I am hourly approaching; and I see around me the raging of fierce passions, threatening the ruin of Church and State. God helping me, I never will yield to popular clamor at the expense of His truth, and of the interests of His church and of my country. May He subdue passion and guide us into His own pure truth.

LECTURE II.

DUTY OF SOUTHERN CHURCHES.

Standing in this place, as a minister of the Lord Jesus Christ, charged with the exposition of His Word, and with the interests of His blood-bought Church, I know no North and no South, no East and no West. These great interests are broad as the earth and vast as eternity; and in view of them, questions of mere sectional interest are to be lost sight of totally. Neither do I know any political party. These interests are destined to live, when all the political parties of to-day are gone and forgotten. They stand infinitely higher than any question of any political party, at any time, in any nation. I belong to no political party. I hold no allegiance to any one of them ; and, therefore, have no temptation to lean one way or another in matters of dispute as between them. Nor am I so unacquainted with human nature as to expect, in the discussion of such questions, and in the midst of such state of feeling as exists in this land, to please everybody. "If I pleased men," said Paul, "I should not be the servant of Christ;" that is, as I suppose, if he aimed to please men, and if he succeeded generally in pleasing them, this fact would be the very best evidence that he did not please his master, Jesus Christ. The Christian minister, under the solemn ordination vows of his office, is not to inquire whether men will be pleased, being charged of God to speak the truth, whether they will hear or forbear.

In the preceding discourse I did not discuss the rightfulness of any slave code, ancient or modern ; but simply the question, whether the Scriptures recognize the relation of master and slave, as one which circumstances have justified, for the time being ; or whether the relation is, *in itself*, sinful, and, therefore always and in all circumstances wrong. I combatted only the extreme position of those who are called Abolitionists. And I may remark here, that I do not use the term as one of reproach ; and I do not suppose it is so considered by those who hold that slaveholding is sinful in itself, or, at least *prima facie* evidence of sin. I have not a word to say in the spirit of denunciation or of reproach. The day has come for calm and kind discussion, not for denunciation.

The definition I gave of slavery, is not my own, but that of eminent moralists, known the world over, and known as well to be opposers of slavery—such men as Paley, Wayland and Chalmers. It is useless to say that the definition is an absurdity, when such names and such authority are given. I defined slavery to be *the obligation on the part of the slave to labor for his master, involving the corresponding obligation on the part of the master to treat him as a man, and to protect all his rights as a man.* The question which I raised and discussed was, whether circumstances have existed which, for the time being, justified good men in sustaining such a relation, governing themselves not by the code of Rome, nor by any other civil code merely, but governing themselves in this relation by the law of God and the directions therein contained. I was very careful to state, still further, in *eight* particulars, what I do, and what I do not, hold to be true in this case—as, for example : That I hold to the *unity* of the human race, that "God hath made of one blood all nations of men for to dwell upon all the face of the earth ;" consequently, in the second place, that the moral law and the golden rule are applicable to all men of all nations and countries ; and thirdly, I hold that slavery is not a *divine institution*, and has never received the *sanction* of God ; still further, that no human being has the right to traffic in his fellow men, either for the sake of gain or for the sake of convenience ; still further, that the marriage tie is sacred, and the marriage of slaves is as valid as that of their masters, so that a man has no more right to separate husband and wife among them, than among others ; still further, that every man has a right to a fair compensation for his labor ; that he has a right to an abundance of food and clothing ; to kind treatment and religious instruction, and to whatever may be fairly his due as a *man ;* still further, that it is the duty of those connected with slavery to elevate their slaves with a view to their freedom, as soon as in the providence of God this can be accomplished. These are the positions I have maintained.

I took no new ground in stating these positions ; for I have, for the last twenty-five years, advocated every one of those principles publicly in the slaveholding and in the free States. I make this statement, because it has been asserted that I dare not advocate those principles in the slaveholding States. These positions, moreover, are fully sustained by the repeated action of the General Assembly of our Church, embracing North and South. I simply stated the doctrine of the Presbyterian Church, nothing more, nothing less. I shall have occasion to quote some, deliverances of our Church, before I get through.

Still further—in undertaking to prove that the relation of master and slave is not necessarily sinful, I did not announce one principle, or give interpretation to any single passage of Scripture, which principle or interpretation has not commanded the assent of the Church of God in all ages, and which does not now command the assent of the great body of wise and good men, the world over. There is no controversy about the interpretation I put upon the passages, among commentators or critics, or those who are admitted to be of authority in the Church of God.

I have presented *three* arguments to show that the relation of master and servant is not *necessarily sinful*. The first is a *presumptive* argument, namely: the fact, that in all ages, for the last eighteen hundred years, the Church of God has understood the Scriptures to teach, that the relation is not necessarily sinful. Dr. Chalmers states, that the doctrine that slave-holding is in itself sinful, "is a factitious and new principle, unknown to the Church of God until within a few years." The second argument was the application of the Golden rule, the principle of which is, that I am bound to improve the condition of my suffering fellow men as far as I can do so consistently with other paramount duties. It could not have been sinful for Christians in the apostolic age to hold slaves, if by so doing they relieved them from exposure to cruel treatment, and even to violent death at the hands of pagan masters. While they might not have been able to emancipate them, they could raise them from the extreme wretchedness and misery in which they lay, and hold them in their own households as servants. The teachings and example of Moses, of Christ and of the Apostles, constituted my third argument; for it is a fact that Moses allowed the relation to be formed, and the Apostles received slaveholders into their Churches without commanding them to manumit their slaves. These facts are admitted by men who declare themselves not only Anti-Slavery, but some of whom glory in the name "Abolitionist."

The conclusion I deduced from these arguments, was not that slaveholding, as it exists in this country, is right or justifiable; but simply *that circumstances have existed, which, for the time being, justified the relation ;* and therefore it is not *in itself* sinful; that since circumstances have existed which justified it, circumstances may again exist to justify it; so that you cannot pronounce slaveholding sinful, without looking at the circumstances. Such was the decision of our General Assembly in 1845.

Now, inasmuch as the rightfulness or wrongfulness of the relation of master and slave depends upon circumstances, the question which I wish to discuss this evening is, *whether the circumstances which now exist in our own country, do so far justify professing Christians, for the time being, in sustaining this relation, that they cannot rightfully be excluded from the Church of God, or denied Church fellowship merely on that account?*

This is the simple question, and it is a question of unspeakable moment. It stands most intimately connected with the peace, and purity, and efficiency, and honor of the Church of God in this land. There may be such a state of corruption in one part of the Church, as would justify another part in refusing to acknowledge them as Christians, and to hold fellowship with them; but until such a state of corruption is shown to exist, we have no right to refuse to hold Christian fellowship with any part of the visible Church. Schism, or the breaking into fragments of the Church of God, is a sin of no ordinary magnitude; and this is not the time to be needlessly rending. Let us examine carefully then upon what ground we may justly say to any portion of the Church of God—"We cannot hold fellowship with you."

It has surprised me very much, in reading so much that has been written on this subject, that no clear statement is attempted of the principles that should determine Christians in relation to fellowship with those differing from them in some particulars. When I was a delegate of the General Assembly to the Consociation of Rhode Island, I raised the question: "What are the principles which control you in this matter?" And there was not a man on the floor who stated any principle at all. Now, it is a very hazardous course to refuse to hold fellowship with professing Christians, without a clear view of the Scripture principles which should control our action.

1. Bear in mind that the question which I discuss, is not whether slavery, as it exists in our own country, had *a righteous*

or an unrighteous origin. I have said that its origin was most
unrighteous. There is no language too strong to be used in
regard to the exceeding sinfulness of the origin of African
slavery, as it exists in our country. The Apostles of the Lord
Jesus Christ, and the early Christians, could not have *established*
Roman slavery, or approved of it; and yet, as a matter of fact,
many of those Christians, living under the civil code of Rome,
did feel themselves at liberty, and probably thought it was their
duty, for the time being, to sustain the relation of masters,
governing their conduct, not by the laws of Rome, but by the
laws of Jesus Christ.

2. The question is not whether the slave code of any government, ancient or modern, is right; whether the slave code of any
one of the Southern States is right. I do not believe that there
is a single slave code in the land that approximates what it ought
to be. Supposing that, for the time being, the existence of
slavery may be justified, still there is not a single State in the
Union whose legislation can be commended, as at all what it
should be. The Apostles and our Lord could not possibly have
enacted the Roman code, or *approved* of it; but they and the
early Christians could live under that code, governing their conduct, not by it, but by the higher law of God. I am sorry to be
obliged to say, I have not a very favorable opinion of the morals
of any one of these United States, or of a great many of the
laws in all these States. I do not believe that the laws of
Illinois approximate perfection. But I have little confidence in
any man whose principles rise no higher, and whose conduct is
no more upright, than the law requires. If any man is disposed
to treat his wife and his children as badly as the civil law will
allow, he is a vile man. No one would deal with a man whose
principles allow him to take every advantage which the civil law
allows. You would refuse to do business with a man whom you
would be obliged to compel by law to comply with his promises.
The Christian man, in all the transactions of life, rises above the
civil code. You cannot protect a man's wife by any civil code.
You cannot prevent men from ill-treating their children by any
system of civil laws. You cannot make men honest by any code
in the world. The great matter for us is to inculcate moral
principles, and to form a public sentiment, that will enforce its
dictates upon the consciences of men. Such a moral principle
and such a public sentiment, are stronger than any civil law in
the world. I am not here to defend civil codes.

3. Consequently the question is not whether there is a great deal of sin connected with slavery—a great deal of suffering and wrong growing out of its existence. Undoubtedly this is true. Unfortunately the people of the South are very much like the people everywhere. There is in human society a great mixture of good and bad, with an unfortunate predominance of the bad. The great majority, alas! of the people of any one of our States cannot be said to be very regardful of God's law. It would be absurd, therefore, to deny that there is a great deal of sin committed in connection with this relation. Is it not so in every relation? Wherever bad men live, they commit bad acts. Wherever bad men have power, they will abuse it. I do not pretend to say, that there is not a great deal of evil growing out of this relation ; but I will venture to say, that the amount of suffering—bodily suffering—connected with it, has been greatly exaggerated. Even bad men are not generally disposed to abuse their horses, but rather take care of them, as a matter of self-interest ; and if a bad man looks upon his slave as he does upon his horse, will he not take care of him for the same reason? The amount of suffering, therefore, as every one acquainted with the South knows, is exaggerated very much. There are great evils in this thing. It originated in wrong, and you never can relieve it from great and dreadful evils ; yet they are not mainly those which are most dwelt upon.

4. Nor am I here to advocate the *perpetuity* of slavery in this country. I have said it was an evil, originating in sin—a great evil, and ought to be abolished just as soon as it can be done, in the circumstances, by the operation of correct principles, and with safety to the parties concerned.

5. Still further—I do hold, that the tendency of the gospel is to abolish slavery ; and it will accomplish the end, if men will let it have fair play. The doctrines and principles of the gospel, pressed upon the hearts and the consciences of men—the providence of God co-operating, will drive it out of our country and the world.

I do not blame any man for hating slavery—for it is a hateful thing, and ought to be hated. I do not wonder that men say hard things about it—especially when so many false or exaggerated statements are constantly published. The thing is evil. I remember, some four years ago, when the General Assembly met in New York, and one of our Congregational brethren—a representative from his Association—spoke of the evil of slavery, the venerable Dr. McFarland, himself a Virginian, who was Moderator of the Assembly, said, in substance, "We don't expect you to approve of it; we do not approve of it ourselves. We regard it as an enormous evil, and we desire to get rid of it." The sentiments he expressed met the approbation of the entire body, South and North.

I do not blame men for not liking slavery. I do not like it myself. I do not plead for the perpetuity of it. I earnestly advocated emancipation in Kentucky twenty-five years ago. I advocated it in the St. Louis *Presbyterian* within the last five years.

I do not propose *now* to discuss the best method of dealing with slavery, *but simply to try to form* an estimate of the character of those Christians living in the Slave States, and of our duty with regard to them. Are they living in such sin that we are bound to reprove them, and cut them off from our fellowship? Is this the view which, in the light of God's word, we ought to take of the matter? I am willing to apply its language, in the strictness of interpretation, to this case. Let us not palliate sin, where it exists; but let us not condemn brethren who are as faithful servants of God, as we.

1. The first question, in examining the circumstances attending the existence of slavery, relates to *the introduction of it into our country*. Upon whom rests the responsibility of its introduction? I raise this question now for this reason: If slavery, as it exists in the slave States, were a matter of their own seeking, then, according to a very obvious principle of civil law, men may not take advantage of their own wrong. If the present slaveholding States brought the difficulty upon themselves, then the responsibility would be greater, and the obligation to remove it at all hazards would be greater. But if it was forced upon them, or if others helped or pushed them into it—then their responsibility would be less.

The first and the great responsibility rests upon Great Britain. Bancroft says: "Before America legislated for herself, the interdict of the slave trade was impossible. England was inexorable in maintaining the system, which gained new and stronger supporters by its excess. English Continental Colonies in the aggregate were always opposed to the African slave trade. Maryland, Virginia, Carolina, each showed an anxious preference for the introduction of white men; and laws designed to restrict the importation of slaves, are scattered copiously all along the records of Colonial legislation." "In Virginia the planters beheld," says Bancroft, "with dismay, the increase of slaves among them."

A letter of Dr. Franklin, dated London, April 28, 1773, mentions a petition sent from the Assembly of Virginia to the British Government for permission to pass laws prohibiting the further importation of slaves into that Colony. "This request," says Franklin, "will probably not be granted. The interests of a few merchants here have more weight with the government than that of thousands at a distance." As a matter of fact it was not granted. Georgia was designed to be free from slavery. It was the determination of Oglethorpe and those associated with him, that slavery never should exist there. He says: "Slavery, the misfortune, if not the dishonor, of other plantations, is absolutely proscribed." This he wrote in 1744. But the English Government forced slavery upon them against their will.

The next responsibility rests upon the States themselves, and upon the North as fully as the South. In the year 1748, the Legislature of New York said: "All due encouragement ought to be given to the direct importation of slaves, and all smuggling of slaves condemned as an eminent discouragement to the fair trader." In 1773, just when Virginia was petitioning the English government for permission to prohibit the further importation of slaves, Newport was the centre of the slave trade, and the wealth of its citizens arose mainly from that source." This is the statement of Rev. Dr. Thompson, one of the editors of the *Independent*, whose prejudices are certainly strongly enough the other way. It was in 1770, the venerable Dr. Hopkins, of New-

mainly in the South. It is amazing that in a country like ours, the slave trade should have been so long sustained.

The very unwilling of the people now living in the slaveholding States, is not that of having made this difference of ... it is an inherited evil, which they now find that in which they came into being. Their obligation is in being encumbered with the evil to apply to it the principles of God's word in their existing circumstances, and to remove it as far and as fast as they can. Under this obligation of christians will end with this evil, to take the word of God as their guide in this matter, and proceed as fast and as that as they can by the removal of these principles. Still the removal ... is a hard task, and every one knows, that a single generation ... to carry a country evils which many generations cannot remove.

2. The duty of Christians in the slave States may be viewed in two aspects. First, as citizens, having a moral influence in moulding public sentiment and having a voice in the legislation of the country. Secondly, they have a responsibility as Christian members of the church of God in relation to the question of holding slaves. These are the two aspects in which a christian and a Christian would view their duty.

The question, then, is this: Is it the duty of ... to ... emancipate their slaves, and to refuse to hold slaves ...

This question can be answered as already intimated, only by looking at the circumstances surrounding them. In considering those circumstances, let us keep in view the moral law of God, and apply its principles, with all severity, if you please, to the facts of the case.

In the first place, it is a fact that in perhaps every one of the Slave States the laws forbid emancipation within ... consequently no man can free his slaves ... Urge Christians in the South instantly to emancipate their slaves, and they will tell you, that it is simply an impossibility—that it cannot be done.

In Kentucky, formerly, the only difficulty in the way of emancipation was, the security required that the emancipated slaves should not be an expense to the State. If a man had but few slaves, the difficulty would not be great; but if he had fifty, or a hundred, or more, he would find difficulty in obtaining the required security. Still many gave the security, and did emancipate their slaves. But this cannot be done now; since the new constitution forbids emancipation in the State.

It is not necessary to prove, that we are not bound to do an impossibility. Consequently it is evidently not the duty of Southern Christians to emancipate their slaves *in the State.*

You may say, that such laws ought not to exist. Admit it; but they do exist; and some of us know, that it is difficult to secure righteous legislation in our own city, in regard to the observance of the Sabbath, for example. It is not easy, where the great majority are not Christians, to repeal bad laws and make good ones.

Do you say, that Southern Christians ought to *remove* their slaves in order to emancipate? The first question they would ask, is, *whither shall we take them?* Will Ohio receive them? If the laws have not been altered since I resided in that State, they require every colored man, within two weeks after coming into the State, to give two resident freeholders as security for his support. Would there be no difficulty in obtaining such security for any considerable number? Indiana has legislated against the settlement of Africans in that State; and even Illinois, with all our boasted freedom, has similar laws! It may be, that these laws are not always or commonly enforced; but, nevertheless, they stand on the statute book, ready to be enforced, if the case demands it. Suppose a slaveholder who has twenty, thirty, fifty, or five hundred slaves, should conclude to purchase lands for them in any part of this State; what would be the result? You can judge, as well as I.

A few years ago, the emancipated slaves of John Randolph were brought into Ohio, and land was purchased for them; but the people of the neighborhood rose up and refused to permit them to be settled amongst them; consequently they were scattered about in different families. I fear, a similar experiment in Illinois would meet with a similar reception. Let us, at least, correct our own legislation, before we condemn that of other States.

But suppose a Southern slaveholder is willing to remove his slaves, and suppose the free States willing to receive them; he encounters another difficulty. His slaves are *intermarried* with those of other men; for generally slaves marry early, and they rarely marry on the plantation where they live. Consequently, the master who would remove his slaves, cannot do so without sundering family ties. He owns a man, but his neighbor owns his wife and children, or he owns the wife and children; and his neighbor owns the husband and father. The slaves are not, and ought not to be, willing to separate for life in order to be free. A friend of my own, who sent his slaves to Liberia, encountered such a difficulty. He owned a woman and her ten children, whilst another man owned the husband and father. He tried to purchase him and offered a high price, but the owner refused to sell. The old man said, "Let my children and my wife go to Liberia, where my children can do well." But when they reached Louisville, the master's heart relented, and he agreed to sell, and immediately the sum was contributed and paid down. I saw the happy family, as they passed through Cincinnati in company with the master and mistress, who accompanied them to Baltimore, and who had provided an ample outfit. In almost every considerable family of slaves, such difficulties would be encountered; and there are great numbers of families owning slaves, who could not, if they would, furnish them with homes in the free States. They cannot do as much for their children. In almost any considerable family of slaves very serious difficulties of this kind would exist. And if they should send their slaves into the free States, what prospect of a comfortable support would they have? I do not wish to magnify the difficulties in the way of emancipation. I simply state facts which every one, so soon as they are stated, must see to be true.

In 1834 a Committee appointed by the Synod of Kentucky, recommended a plan of emancipation, containing the following recommendations, viz:

1. We would recommend that all slaves now under twenty years of age, and all those yet to be born in our possession, be emancipated, as they severally reach their twenty-fifth year.

2. We recommend that deeds of emancipation be now drawn up and recorded in our respective County Courts, specifying the slaves we are about to emancipate, and the age at which each is to become free.

3. We recommend that our slaves be instructed in the common elementary branches of education.

4. We recommend that strenuous and persevering efforts be made to induce them to attend regularly upon the ordinary services of religion, both domestic and public.

5. We recommend that great pains be taken to teach them
the Holy Scriptures, and that to effect this the instrumentality
of Sabbath Schools, whenever they can be enjoyed, be united
with that of domestic instruction.

Such was the plan recommended—a plan which I—then a
member of that Synod—cordially supported. But how long was
it before this outside interference on the part of the Abolitionists
defeated the whole thing? And now, within a few years, the
State of Kentucky has adopted a Constitution which forbids
emancipation, without removal of the slaves emancipated from
the State.

Do you say, then, *colonize them in Africa?* Yes, our General
Assembly has again and again recommended the colonization
enterprise; but our Abolitionist friends made violent opposition
to it, almost as soon as it was fairly under way. Garrison
initiated this movement by publishing most serious charges
against it, as a great pro-slavery concern. Others, and among
them many ministers of the Gospel, united with him in this
opposition, and a great many of the former friends of colonization drew off from it, and became active opposers of it. The
consequence was, that the enterprise was very nearly ruined.
And to this day it receives but a very limited support in the free
States. So that if a large number of slaves should be emancipated, great difficulty would be experienced in securing the
necessary funds, unless far greater liberality should be shown
than heretofore.

I have long believed that the colonization enterprise is one of
the most glorious enterprises of the nineteenth century; and
one of the most serious charges I feel bound to make against the
Abolitionists, is their strange and unaccountable opposition to
this great enterprise, fraught with so many blessings to the
African race. And since they were so greatly in the wrong in
their estimate of the colonization scheme, and in their opposition
to it, it becomes them to be somewhat modest now in denouncing
the Presbyterian Church, which stood firmly by the Society in
its trials, and sustained it against their unreasonable and unrighteous opposition. And now that they see their error, let
them give Presbyterians the credit which is their due.

But Christian masters find difficulty in sending their slaves to
Liberia, in consequence of a prevailing prejudice amongst them

against going to a foreign land, of which they have heard so many unfavorable stories, and of which they really know so little. They are ignorant and timid, and very naturally shrink from what seems to them so great and difficult an undertaking.

A still further difficulty is experienced, as in the case of removal to the free States, from the intermarriages of slaves owned by different persons. A slaveholder desires to send his slaves to Liberia; but they are intermarried with the slaves of other men. Consequently he cannot send them without sundering family ties, to which they would not and should not consent. Some slaveholders can, in this way, secure freedom to their slaves; and, indeed, many have done it; but the large majority probably cannot do it, if they would. But suppose a cotton planter, for example, has principle and zeal enough in this matter to emancipate all his slaves. He has a cotton plantation with the usual number of slaves. When he has emancipated them, he must sell his farm, and remove to some other place, and engage in other business. It requires no ordinary amount of moral principle and of zeal for the welfare of slaves to make so great a sacrifice. The number of men is small in any part of the world, who would exhibit such a degree of disinterested benevolence. Nevertheless, under the influence of the Gospel, many good men had sacrificed a fortune in order to place their slaves where they would be truly free. Still, until the standard of piety shall rise higher than it now is in any part of our country, the number who will make such sacrifices, will be comparatively small.

The indisputable facts demonstrate, that while some slaveholders can emancipate their slaves, the very large majority cannot do it, however they might desire it. It is, therefore, absurd to demand, as a condition of Christian fellowship, that they should do it.

I say nothing at all in regard to the question, whether it would be of advantage to the slaves to be emancipated and to remain amongst the whites. It is certainly true, as demonstrated by history, that the conflict between different races has resulted in the fiercest and most deadly strife known amongst men. Whether two races so different, the one so degraded, with so little sympathy, could live together on any terms of equality, without perpetual conflicts, you can judge as well as I. I am not authorized, as a minister of Jesus Christ, to give any decision on such a question.

I have said nothing as to whether the slaves are *satisfied* in their condition. The fact is, I have seen very few satisfied people in this world. I have not found a great many in this place. It would be strange, if the slaves had so little human nature as to be satisfied, when all the rest of mankind are discontented. I have little doubt, if the matter were presented to them, and if they had an opportunity to choose between freedom and slavery, they would generally prefer freedom. This is simply saying, that they are *men*. In ordinary circumstances I would say with Paul, " If thou mayest be free, choose it rather."

The difficulties attending the question of emancipation, are undoubtedly great; and in determining the duty of Southern Christians, the question is pertinent, whether there were greater difficulties in the way of emancipation in the Apostolic churches? So far as I can ascertain, there was no law in the Roman Empire against emancipating slaves. If there was any such law, it has yet to be produced. My impression is, there was no such law. There must have been circumstances to justify the relation of master and slave, or the Apostles would have required Christians to emancipate. But it is certain that the difficulties in the way of emancipation now, are as great, to say the least, as they were in the Apostolic age. How can you, then, come, in the face of the fact, which is admitted by leading Abolitionists, by Dr. Wayland and Dr. Chalmers, that the Apostles did not require emancipation, and make this demand of Southern Christians, when there are difficulties in their way at least as great as those existing in the Apostolic age? Dr. Chalmers, and Dr. Tyler, of East Windsor Theological Seminary, take the ground, that in making such a demand, you do it in the face of the teachings and the example of the Apostles of Christ.

Do you say, it is their duty to seek to change the laws of the States in which they reside? Admit it; then the question arises —How ought they to go to work to produce this effect? You ask them to change their laws. Where the people frame the laws, to effect any favorable change in them, you must change the public sentiment, and get the majority in favor of the change —a permanent majority; otherwise there will be a re-action, and the laws be made worse than before. How are Christians to go to work at this thing?

You can scarcely say, that the Bible prescribes the mode in which such a thing ought to be done. They must, therefore, decide for themselves.

Let us look at facts. How was it in the State of Kentucky? There was, a few years ago, a better prospect of securing laws in favor of emancipation in that State, than in any other—if we except, perhaps, Maryland and Missouri. Leading men in the State were in favor of it. Henry Clay says, in one of his speeches, that he labored for this thing many years ago, and failed.

Within ten years, a new Constitution was adopted in Kentucky, and the question was raised respecting emancipation. It came up in the form of what was called "The Open Clause" in the Constitution, admitting of Emancipation. What were the facts? The Presbyterians generally favored "The Open Clause;" and several prominent ministers did what I had not known Presbyterian ministers to do before—they discussed the question through the State. Dr. Young, the able President of Centre College, held a public discussion at Danville, with a politician, in which he advocated emancipation, with great ability. Some expressed the opinion that the Institution would be injured, for it was patronized largely from the South. But the result was widely different. Dr. Robert J. Breckinridge, now principal Professor in the Danville Theological Seminary in Kentucky, ran as the emancipation candidate for the Convention, and, to use a common phrase, stumped it through the District, exposing the evils of slavery. But he was not elected. Presbyterians through the State, so far as I can learn, generally took this ground. I took occasion, at that time, though residing in Cincinnati, to publish a letter in Kentucky, urging emancipation. The other leading denominations did not sustain us in this effort. The Methodist Church was divided, and very naturally the South church went to the other extreme. A leading Baptist minister ran as a pro-slavery candidate against the Hon. Thos. F. Marshall, and was elected. And strangely enough, many men not holding slaves, opposed emancipation, because the slaves, it was said, would be placed on an equality with them! It was not only the slaveholding, but the non-slaveholding portion of the community, that defeated the cause of emancipation. The result was, that instead of getting a Constitution favorable to emancipation, one was adopted that totally forbids it. I am not sure that many of our Abolition friends here have heard of these things. If any one in Kentucky had greatly abused his slaves, they would probably have heard the news. Let the whole truth be known, and let the Presbyterians have due credit.

There would be much greater difficulty in other Southern States, in effecting any change in the laws in favor of emancipation; and the very first effort to effect any such change, especially in the present state of feeling, would merely aggravate the evil. The cause of this state of feeling may appear hereafter; the fact of its existence is painfully evident.

It is, moreover, a fact, that many of the wisest and most earnest friends of emancipation of the slaves, believe that any plan of emancipation *without colonization*, would do more harm than good. Henry Clay is known to have been opposed to slavery, and he threw his great influence in favor of gradual emancipation. Let me quote a sentence or two from a speech of his before the Colonization Society.

Said Mr. Clay:—" If I could be instrumental in eradicating this deepest stain upon the character of our country, and removing all cause of reproach on account of it by foreign nations—if I could be instrumental in ridding of this foul blot the revered State that gave me birth, or that not less beloved State which kindly adopted me as her son, I would not exchange the proud satisfaction which I should enjoy, for all the triumphs ever decreed to the most successful conqueror."

And yet he said:—" If the question was submitted, whether there should be immediate or gradual emancipation of all the slaves of the United States without their removal or colonization, painful as it is to express the opinion, I have no doubt that it would be unwise to emancipate them. For I believe that the aggregate of the evils which would be engendered in society, upon the supposition of such general emancipation, and of the liberated slaves remaining among us, would be greater than all the evils of slavery, great as they unquestionably are."

Such was the opinion of that eminent man; and it is the prevailing opinion in the South. All efforts there to get a change of laws in favor of emancipation without colonization, must be fruitless. Such are the difficulties now existing. And certainly we have no right to censure the feeling, so long as we ourselves cherish it.

An able writer in the South, in an article on this subject, has charged upon us our inconsistency. "You of the North who reprove us," he remarks in substance, "make laws against a few straggling blacks, who come amongst you, and yet ask us to turn loose three or four millions of them in our midst!" It would be difficult to answer this retort. For Christians at the South to attempt such a change in the laws, as we have supposed, would be eminently unwise. Such a course would only prevent those improvements in the laws which may be secured.

What, then, ought our Southern brethren and our Church do? Do you say, let them, if they cannot free their slaves legally, recognize them as *men*, and apply the golden rule in their treatment of them? I agree with you heartily. You will not contend, however, that they must have the responsibility of maintaining their slaves, without requiring them to labor. This would be most unreasonable. No man should be held responsible for persons whom he cannot control. If held legally responsible, the master must have the right of control; or he is a slave to the servant. But in the exercise of authority, let them treat them as men, guided by the Divine law.

Such precisely is the doctrine of the Presbyterian Church. Dr. Thompson maintains, that while the Apostles did not abolish slavery, they lifted it up from the plane of the Civil law to the higher plain of the Gospel law. Now, suppose the Presbyterian Church has done the same thing.

Let me read an extract from the action of the General Assembly of 1818. That body speaks of "the practice into which Christian people have most inconsistently fallen, of enslaving a portion of their *brethren* of mankind. For that 'God hath made of one blood all nations of men for to dwell on all the face of the earth." This is precisely in accordance with my position. Do you say, this doctrine could not be preached in the South? This document was adopted unanimously. Dr. Baxter, of Virginia, was a member of the committee that reported it. The Assembly further urge the Churches to endeavor "to obtain the complete abolition of slavery throughout Christendom, and if possible, throughout the world." Is not this strong enough?

It may be said, this paper was adopted many years ago. I answer, it was re-affirmed in 1846 by both the North and the South, unanimously—and again in 1850. In the resolution of

1846 the Assembly said in substance, that for sixty years the
General Assemblies have been uttering the same sentiments,
which can be proved by the word of God. In a speech in the
last General Assembly, in Indianapolis, I declared that I hold
the doctrine of the paper of 1818 to be true to the letter. And
yet I was elected with extraordinary unanimity to a Professorship
in the Theological Seminary of the Northwest. What evidence
is there, then, that the church has changed her ground?

In 1845, the General Assembly received several petitions from
Abolitionists to exclude all slaveholders from the Church. The
Assembly decided, that they could not exclude any one from the
Church, as a slaveholder, without looking at the circumstances.
In that document, which I had the honor of drafting, the following language is found : " We exhort every believing master to
remember that his Master is also in heaven, and in view of all
the circumstances in which he is placed, to act in the spirit of
the Golden Rule, ' Whatsoever ye would that men should do
to you, do ye even so to them." Such was the ground taken
in 1845, and every Southern member voted for it. About
thirteen from the North did not.

Do you say, that the church ought to go farther, and forbid the
traffic in men, and the separation of husbands and wives. This
has been done. Let me read the law of our church on that point.
The General Assembly of 1818 used the following language :

" We enjoin it on all church Sessions and Presbyteries under
the care of this Assembly, to discountenance, and as far as
possible, to prevent all cruelty of whatever kind in the treatment
of slaves; especially the cruelty of separating husband and wife,
parents and children, and that which consists in selling slaves to
those who will either themselves deprive these unhappy people
of the blessings of the gospel, or will transport them to places
where the Gospel is not proclaimed, or where it is forbidden to
slaves to attend upon its institutions. The manifest violation or
disregard of the injunction, here given, in its true spirit and
intention, ought to be considered a just ground for the discipline
and censures of the Church. And if it shall ever happen that a
Christian professor in our communion shall sell a slave, who is
also in communion and good standing in the church, contrary to
his or her will and inclination, it ought immediately to claim the
particular attention of the church judicatories; and unless there
be such peculiar circumstances attending the case as can but

seldom happen, it ought to be followed without delay by a
suspension of the offender from all the privileges of the church,
till he repent and make all the reparation in his power to the
injured party."

Such is the law of the Presbyterian Church.

The Assembly of 1845 used the following language: "The
Assembly are not to be understood as denying that there is evil
connected with slavery. Much less do they approve those
defective and oppressive laws by which in some of the States it
is regulated. Nor would they by any means countenance the
traffic in slaves for the sake of gain; the separation of husbands
and wives, parents and children, for the sake of 'filthy lucre' or
for the convenience of the master; or cruel treatment of slaves
in any respect. Every Christian and philanthropist certainly
should seek, by all peaceable and lawful means, the repeal of
unjust or oppressive laws, and the amendment of such as are
defective, so as to protect the slaves from evil treatment by
wicked men, and secure to them the right to receive religious
instruction."

Do you say, the Church should go further, and condemn the
mere chattelism of human beings? Let me read again: "Nor
is this Assembly to be understood as countenancing the idea, that
masters may regard their servants as *mere property* and not as
human beings, rational, accountable, immortal. The Scriptures
prescribe not only the duties of servants, but also of masters,
warning the latter to discharge those duties, knowing that their
Master is in heaven, neither is there respect of persons with
him."

Is not this language strong enough?

It may be asked whether the Presbyterian churches at the
South, regard this injunction? Let me read you one out of a
great number of evidences I could give you upon this subject.
The pastoral letter of the Presbytery of Tombigbee, of Missis-
sippi, after referring to the repeated action of the General
Assembly, states, that "many of our best and ablest ministers have
devoted themselves, in whole or in part, to special labor for the
salvation of these people; and our Southern churches, presbyteries and synods, are yearly showing an increased interest and
watchfulness in regard to it." Again: "Among our own churches
this presbytery is glad to know and record the fact that religious
privileges are enjoyed by the servants in very many places, in

common with their masters, such as to leave them without
excuse. And several of our churches report a large colored
membership, even equal to, or larger, than the membership of
whites.   *   *   *   *   *   *   *

"The moral law is the absolute rule of moral duty, and so also
it is the charter of human rights. It is the right of every human
being, prince, subject and citizen, parents and children, masters
and servants, to obey the law of God. No government in the
commonwealth, or in the household, can be called anything less
than unrighteous, which denies to any of God's intelligent
creatures the right of obeying those moral commands, or which
inhibits the free exercise of that right. One of the very highest
duties of the master, in rendering to his servants that which is
just and equal, is to secure for them the right and opportunity to
worship and obey God, to protect them in the free exercise, and
encourage them in the constant practice thereof.   *   *   *
"Be careful to protect them in the enjoyment of the rights, and
encourage them in the duties of the family. The chiefest of
these is that of marriage. Unfortunately the law does not throw
its protection around them in this behalf; although public sentiment, which is nearly as powerful as law, does. But, still,
sometimes by removals and deaths, occasions of hardship under
this head occur, although we hope not among you. And yet, so
sacred are these rights to your servants, and so debasing must be
any denial of them, that we feel it to be our duty to put you on
your guard, and renewedly to invoke your diligence, exhorting
you rather to suffer pecuniary damage yourselves, than to allow
moral wrong to accrue to your servants. Did they know that
they were absolutely protected from wrong in the wanton
dissevering of the tie of marriage, they would value it more and
cherish it with more constancy. Again, encourage them in the
discharge of proper parental duties towards their children—
especially whenever they seem to estimate their responsibilities
aright, and aim to discharge them on Christian principles.
Encourage them, also, where the parents are pious, to hold domestic worship; which is, of itself one of the primary Christian
duties, and besides, it is one of the surest means of confirming
the family tie, and one of the divinely appointed means of training
children to the practice of righteousness and the knowledge of
salvation. And then, not only grant them the right, but urge

them to embrace the privilege of presenting their children for Christian baptism. By these means much may be done to rescue the family tie from neglect, to make them value its privileges and enjoy its blessings.

This language speaks for itself.

Slaves are not only treated as men, but those that are pious, have the right to present their children for baptism. I have myself repeatedly baptised the children of slaves, and many other ministers have done the same. Now, will any one, in view of these documents, say, that Presbyterians regard their servants as *mere tools, with souls in them?* I have quoted the action of but one Southern Presbytery. I could read you by the hour from other Presbyteries and Synods. It is a well-known fact that many of our ministers have devoted themselves particularly to the instruction of the slaves, among whom I may mention Dr. C. C. Jones, who, while laboring for the blacks, was called to a Theological Professorship. After filling the Professorship for a time, he returned to his former work. I prefer giving the testimony of others rather than my own. Some years ago, when I labored in Cincinnati, Rev. Mr. King, of Canada, who has long been engaged in laboring among the fugitive slaves, and who had been South, and inherited through his wife several slaves, and who was then removing them to Canada, delivered an address in my church, in which he stated the course pursued by our church in the South, and, with all his anti-slavery feelings, he said, instead of finding fault with Presbyterians of the South, they ought to be encouraged in their work, since they were doing all they could in ameliorating the condition of the slaves. Such was the testimony of a man then devoted to the anti-slavery cause, and now devoting his time to the fugitives. He had the opportunity to be correctly informed, for he had labored in the South several years.

Let me lay before you the testimony of the Reverend Dr. Humphrey, so long President of Amherst College, father of the respected pastor of one of the churches in this city.

"Many masters and mistresses spend much of the Sabbath in giving them (the slaves) moral and religious instruction, which is greatly blessed to them." Again: "But a few, in the free States, I believe, are aware to what an extent the owners of large plantations at the South are co-operating with religious societies in bringing their slaves under the sound of the Gospel, nor of its saving effects upon tens of thousands who hear it. In the cities, congregations and churches of colored people, mostly slaves, have been gathered by themselves and under pastors of their own kindred. Elsewhere, slaves and their masters worship and sit together at the Lord's table. The Spirit of the Lord is poured out upon the bond as well as the free, if not more copiously. I had no idea myself, till lately, how much is doing in the slave States for the blacks, nor of the success of missionary labors among them.''

He gives, in the same connection, a statement of the number of colored members in different churches, as well as of missionaries employed amongst them.

I do not stand on the defensive here. I venture to say, to the honor of my church, that no other church has gone so far, or done so much, to promote emancipation. I can demonstrate that the Presbyterian church has emancipated more slaves than all the Abolitionists in this land. I am ready to compare notes on this subject, at any time.

We have not made so much noise, perhaps; nor have the emancipated slaves gone to Canada. They have either been emancipated in the States, before the laws forbade it, or have gone to Liberia. We have not stood at a distance and passed hard resolutions, or published hard sayings. We have stood on the ground and made our influence felt amongst slaveholders. We have advocated emancipation, where there seemed a prospect of promoting it.

I stated, last Sabbath, that slavery existed many years in New England, and that it was never, TO ANY EXTENT, made matter of discipline by the churches, until abolished by the civil law. I observe, in one of the city papers, that some one signing himself "New England," denies the correctness of my statement. Allow me to say, that I never make statements upon such subjects without knowing them to be correct. He refers to the Rev. Dr. Hopkins, who attacked the slave trade in Newport, and states that in 1784 he made slaveholding a matter of discipline, and in 1785 several other churches had freed themselves from this thing. The fact which he denies, I stated in my "Ten Letters to the Delegates of the Congregational Association of New England," some five years ago, and asked them to say whether it was true, and it was not denied. Four years ago, I stated the same fact before the Consociation of Rhode Island, while the successor of Dr. Hopkins was present, and it was not denied.

It was not more than ten years ago, that Dr. Bacon introduced a resolution into the Association of Connecticut, recommending the churches to commence discipline with those members implicated in slaveholding. Ten years ago, there were known to be slaveholders in good standing in the churches in Connecticut. Still further, it is only fifteen years ago, that Dr. Tyler, the venerable Professor in East Windsor Theological Seminary, used this language: "They (the Abolitionists) denounce us as pro-slavery, because we will not shut our pulpits against Southern ministers. But the Bible will not justify them in the ground they take. The great Head of the Church communed with such men as many of the Southern Christians are, and I will not refuse to do it." The venerable Professor was neither removed nor censured. The same ground is taken by others. So, you see, New England is not yet converted to the new doctrines.

When the question in regard to correspondence with our Assembly was before the Consociation of Rhode Island, it was decided negatively by a bare majority. One of the oldest ministers of that body said, that the Presbyterian Church was doing more than all the Abolitionists together for the benefit of the slaves. The Rev. Dr. Thayer said, eloquently, that if the Government were broken into fragments, he would still stretch his arm across and shake hands with his brethren. And even after I had discussed this subject in New England, I received a letter from a distinguished Congregational minister, inquiring whether I would encourage the Board of Directors of one of their Theological Seminaries to elect me to a Professorship. New England is not yet converted, or no one there would have desired me to teach theology for them.

It is not long since Dr. Lord, the venerable President of Dartmouth College, published two pamphlets more pro-slavery than anything I ever published, and he is there still in good standing. Rev. Dr. Stiles, also once a slaveholder, and who has recently published a book against Abolitionism, was for several years pastor of a Congregational Church in New Haven. Even the Associate Reformed Brethren have not been able to carry

out the Abolitionist doctrines in the South. The Methodist
Church North, has not done it. They are still agitated, and
likely to divide again. If it is so hard to convert men in the
North, is it strange that Southern Christians are not converted
to Abolitionism? The old adage is applicable here: "First cast
out the beam out of thine own eye, and then shalt thou see
clearly to cast out the mote out of thy brother's eye."

But the question returns: What ought our brethren of the
South to do? and what ought the Presbyterian Church to do?
In my Ten Letters to the Congregational delegates, I said in
substance, "We have examined this matter carefully, and we
think we are right; if you have any light, we would be glad to
receive it. What ought we to do?" One of them intimated to
me that they would probably answer the Letters, if they did not
like them, after having examined them; but they have never
done so.

Again, four years ago, I presented the same question to the
Consociation of Rhode Island. I said substantially: "Brethren,
we want light. If we are guilty, our sin is one of omission or
commission; which is it? What is your charge? Can you tell us
what we ought to do?"

Not a man on that floor attempted to say what our sin was, or
what our duty. And when I took my leave of them, after the
passage of the resolution cutting off the correspondence with us,
I said to them in substance: "I shall be obliged to report to
the General Assembly, that not a man of you ventured to say
what is the sin that has led you discourteously to terminate a
correspondence sought by yourselves." The Moderator stated
that he had intended to vote with the majority, but in view of
what he had heard, he must cast his vote the other way.

The Boston *Recorder*, which I believe to be the most ably
edited religious paper in New England, took up this matter,
after the discussions were published, and in view of my challenge
in the "Ten Letters" and before the Consociation, made the
following remarks: "This suggestion we are fairly bound to
meet. If they are doing in all respects what the great law of
beneficence and right requires, our complaints fall harmless at
their feet. We would that some of those acute minds that have
made slavery the subject of much study, would turn their reflec-
tions mainly upon this point. We would that the subject should
be viewed rather in the concrete than in the abstract; that we

should take the facts as they are, and in a full and candid view of them decide the Christians now in the position of slaveholders at the South, may be fairly required to do. Until that is done, nothing will be done towards any desirable change in the action of slaveholders and in the condition of the slaves. We must confess that so far as our observation extends, this point has been too much avoided."

It is true, as the *Recorder* says, this point has been *too much avoided*. That is, those friends of ours, who have been condemning our church, have been heaping reproach upon us without being able to specify any sin, or tell us what we ought to do! The call of the Boston *Recorder* has met no response, even though the appeal was made to the most acute minds of New England. Why do they not respond? However humble in myself, I spoke as the representative of the General Assembly, and in the name of that venerable body I made the call. No answer has been made to this hour—no attempt at an answer has been made. Is it not strange? I have been denounced as pro-slavery, and the Church has been denounced as pro-slavery, and for five years this challenge has been before the public, and not a man has been bold enough to answer it. I venture boldly to defy any one to answer it.

The question recurs—What ought the Presbyterian Church to do? If these gentlemen cannot tell, after so many years of agitation, it must be a difficult matter. Shall we cut off all these Southern brethren, when their Northern brethren, the very men who reprove them, cannot tell what they ought to do?

Finally, I hold communion with my Southern brethren, as well as my Northern brethren, *because God has owned the one as distinctly as he has the other, by his special blessing upon their labors.* He has been with not only the Presbyterian Church as a church, but with the churches in the South. We have a Bible test by which to settle this question. When the Saviour gave sight to a blind man, the Pharisees said: "We know that God spake unto Moses: as for this fellow, we know not whence he is." He made the following conclusive answer: "Now we know that God heareth not sinners, but if any man be a worshipper of God and doeth his will, him God heareth." When Peter received Cornelius and his family into the church, and was called to account for it, he answered: "Forasmuch then as God gave

them the like gift as he did to us who believed in the Lord Jesus
Christ, what was I that I could withstand God?" The Holy
Spirit was poured out upon them; and for Peter to refuse to
acknowledge them, would have been to withstand God! Here
is a Bible test. Is it true then that God has heard the prayers
of Southern Christians? Has the Holy Spirit set his seal upon
the Gospel, as his servants preach it there? Hear the testimony
of a gentleman of high standing, who will be deemed good
authority by most Abolitionists. The Rev. Dr. Stowe, of
Andover, says: "I know individuals who are slaveholders, and
particular churches which include slaveholders, whom, according
to all the evidence I can gather, Christ does accept, and those
individuals and those particular churches, on my principles, I
cannot reject and I will not. This is true ground—" God
heareth not sinners."

It cannot be denied, that the churches in the slaveholding
States have enjoyed many powerful revivals of religion, and that
the Gospel preached amongst them is the power of God to
salvation to multitudes of souls. Not a few of the ablest ministers in the different denominations, if ever truly converted, were
converted in such churches. This is true, for example, of the
late Dr. A. Alexander, for forty years an honored Professor in
our oldest Theological Seminary, the beloved and venerated
instructor of a large portion of our ministers. It is true of Dr.
Daniel Baker, who, for many years, was wonderfully honored of
God, as an instrument in the conversion of men, and whose
successful labors were mainly in the South.

For myself, if I know anything of the religion of the heart, I
experienced the change in a church in a slaveholding State, in
a glorious revival. For a number of years, I exercised my
ministry in churches containing slaveholders, and was permitted
to rejoice in many powerful revivals. I witnessed the same
awakenings, the same struggles under conviction, the same
humble trust in Christ, the same reformation, the same joy in
young converts, which I have seen in churches in the free States;
and I saw the same earnest desire for the progress of Christ's
cause, the same agonizing prayers, the same Christian liberality,
the same self-denial, which I have seen elsewhere. I have been
with those Christians through all the varieties of temptation,
losses, bereavements, sicknesses and sufferings; and I have stood
by their death-beds, poured the precious promises into their

ears, and witnessed their triumphant departure from this world.
Some of the most triumphant deaths I ever witnessed, occurred
amongst them. I have sometimes felt, as if I would gladly
travel a thousand miles to witness such triumphs of grace again.
If I have not seen genuine and powerful revivals amongst them,
I have never seen revivals anywhere. If those churches are not
true churches of Christ, I know none that are.

Will you ask me to refuse to acknowledge as my brother, those
whom God has acknowledged as his children? Shall I refuse to
commune with those in whom the Holy Spirit dwells, and with
whom my Saviour holds fellowship! The very idea seems to me
impious. Who are we, that we should refuse to hold communion
with those whom God has called into His kingdom, whose
prayers he answers, whose labors he blesses, and with whom he
condescends to dwell?

It is a sweeping doctrine, which is urged upon us by Abolitionists. It not only cuts off all the churches and Christian people
of the South, as unworthy of confidence; but it equally cuts off
the Puritans of New England—such men as President Edwards,
and a multitude more. It sweeps away the New England
churches, all of which were, directly or indirectly, involved in the
sin of slavery. The moral law, the teachings and examples of
Christ and his Apostles, and the witness of the Holy Spirit—all
forbid us to believe the doctrine, or to submit to the demands of
Abolitionists.

From its earliest commencement in this country, the Presbyterian Church has occupied substantially the same ground, not
"tossed to and fro by every wind of doctrine." Her first
utterance, on the subject of slavery, date as far back as the year
1787. The paper then adopted by the Synod of Philadelphia
and New York (for the General Assembly was not yet organized)
exhorted the members of the churches to give those slaves such
education as would fit them for freedom. From that day to this,
all the utterances of our church have been of the same character.
True, some few ministers, and others, in the North, have been
disposed to take extreme positions in one direction, and some in
the South have had leanings in the opposite direction. But the
church, as a body, has never changed her position; and, I trust,
she never will.

Allow me to say, in conclusion, if I believed that the tendency
of Abolitionism was to remove slavery from our country, it would

D

at once rise many degrees in my estimation. But after the most
careful examination, I am compelled to believe, that, whilst it
divides churches and imperils the interests of the country, it
tends strongly to perpetuate slavery, and to aggravate all its
evils. I do most sincerely believe, that the course pursued by
the Presbyterian Church does tend most effectually to meliorate
the condition of the slaves, to prepare them for freedom, and to
effect their emancipation, whenever in the providence of God,
emancipation shall be practicable. All this and more I expect to
prove in my next lecture.

LECTURE III.

THE TRUE MODE OF DEALING WITH SLAVERY.

The discussion of the subject of slavery thus far, has related exclusively to the question respecting the Christian character of those churches that stand connected with it, and the treatment which they ought to receive at the hands of their brethren. This discussion involves two important inquiries. First. Whether slaveholding is *sin in itself*—sin under all circumstances; because if it be so, it would follow that all slaveholders are living in sin, and ought, therefore, to be subjected to the discipline of the church, so far as they are members of the church. The second question is this: Since slaveholding is not in itself sinful, but the sinfulness of it depends upon circumstances; do circumstances now exist in this country, which justify Christians, for the time being, in sustaining this relation; so that they cannot properly be excluded from membership in the Church of Christ?

I think I have proved, that slaveholding is not necessarily sinful, but that the moral character of it depends upon circumstances; and I think I have shown, that the circumstances attending its existence in our country, are such as to justify many Christian people in sustaining the relation of masters, for the time being; and consequently, we cannot, on Scriptural ground, refuse to hold fellowship with the churches in the slaveholding States. I now propose to discuss the following question :

What is the true method of treating slavery, as it exists in our country, so as most effectually to mitigate its evils, whilst it continues, and so as most speedily and safely to abolish it?

This question is one of infinite importance, involving not only the duty of the Church of Christ towards nearly four millions

of our fellow creatures, but the interests of them and their
descendants for generations to come. On such a question it is
undoubtedly true, that good men may differ, though equally
anxious to do what is wisest and best. Two physicians, equally
anxious for the recovery of a patient, may differ very materially
respecting the best mode of treatment. Two statesmen, equally
patriotic, may differ widely respecting the best means of promoting the interests of their country, in any important crisis. And
here I cannot but notice a most serious blunder on the part of
Abolitionists. It has been their habit to condemn as pro-slavery
every one who ventures to differ from them, either respecting
the character of Christian slaveholders, or respecting the best
method of treating the evil. Thus they have placed multitudes
of the best men and the warmest friends of the slaves, in the
pro-slavery ranks. " I do hope," said Dr. Chalmers, " that this
obtrusive spirit of theirs will have an effectual check put upon
it; it impedes, besides, the very object which their own hearts
are set upon, and which there are other hearts, as zealous, but
only somewhat wiser, which are as much set upon as theirs."
No procedure can be more unwise, in the effort to accomplish a
great and difficult object, than to throw the influence of men
against it, who are aiming at the same result, by adopting
measures they cannot approve, and then denouncing them for
refusing to co-operate. It is infinitely better to concede something to the conscientious convictions of others, in order to
adopt a platform on which all friendly to the object can stand
and work together.

That I may not be misunderstood, I wish, at the outset, to say
a word regarding the question now so seriously agitating the
country, viz: the extension of slavery into the Territories.
Respecting the questions disputed between the two great political parties, I have nothing to say. The pulpit is not the place
to express opinions on mere political issues. But I am very free
to say—that, regarding slavery as a great evil, I should be sorry
to see it extended over any new territory; and were I a citizen
in such a territory, I would certainly exert any moral influence I
could properly command, to exclude it; and, as a citizen, I
should cast my vote in the same way.

Having thus stated my views on this point, that I may not be
misapprehended, I proceed to state a great principle, of which
Christians should never lose sight, viz: Divine grace and Divine

providence are the two great agencies by which the Divine purposes, in relation to mankind, are fulfilled. These are the wheel within a wheel, that Ezekiel saw. Divine grace operates through God's revealed truth, ordinarily taught through the instrumentality of His church, enlightening the minds, quickening the consciences, and renewing the hearts of men, and thus turning them to righteousness. By its influence the views and principles of individuals are changed, communities are moulded, and ultimately, the legislation of States is improved. The church is the salt of the earth, the light of the world.

Divine providence is sovereign, using human instrumentality or not, as God pleases. Its movements are often too deep and too high for human comprehension. "Thy judgments," saith the Psalmist, "are a great deep." Even the wisest men are often troubled in the attempt to comprehend the ways of God. Contemplating the dispersion of the Jews, God's ancient people, the Apostle Paul exclaims—"O the depth of the riches both of the wisdom and knowledge of God! How unsearchable are His judgments, and his ways past finding out."

In the accomplishment of His purposes, God has assigned to His church a most important instrumentality. It is hers to "go teach all nations"—to impress Divine truth on the minds of men, and pray for the efficacious agency of the Holy Spirit. In doing this she has accomplished the whole work which her Saviour has committed to her hands. Then let her wait for and watch the openings and leadings of Divine Providence, in relation to those things in which that Providence is especially concerned. It was a hard bondage which the Jews endured in Egypt; but there was no earthly power that could have delivered them, till the end of the four hundred and thirty years, appointed by God. He had great purposes to answer by having them detained in captivity in Babylon just seventy years; and no earthly power could have hastened their return to their own land. And it is an instructive fact, that the false prophets were continually exciting them to insubordination by promises of speedy deliverance; whilst Jeremiah was greatly reproached for bidding them be quiet, peaceful and prayerful, till the time appointed of God. Many of our modern prophets imitate those who troubled Jeremiah and the Jews; and we see the fruits of their folly.

Now, although we have no revelation of the purposes of God to be accomplished by permitting the existence of African slavery in our country, or of the period when it is to end; yet no one who believes in the doctrine of Divine providence, can doubt—that God has great purposes to be accomplished by means of it. We cannot suppose, that whilst he guides the flight, and protects the life of a sparrow, till it has accomplished the end of its being, he has left to mere accident or to the passions of men, the introduction and continuance of slavery in our country. And if he has purposes to accomplish in connection with it; then none can remove it more rapidly, than will be the ripening of those purposes. Already do we see some light on this dark subject. Great as was the wickedness of those who, for filty lucre, tore the Africans from their native country, and sold them into slavery; many and terrible as have been the evils involved in its existence; it is still true, to the praise of Divine grace, that hundreds of thousands of them have become the disciples of Christ, and are now rejoicing in heaven; and hundreds of thousands more are on their way to join them. It is true, likewise, to the praise of Divine goodness, that many of them have been enabled by Christian and philanthropic men to return to Africa, bearing with them Christianity and a Christian civilization— diffusing light and blessing over that dark continent. What other and further purposes God has to accomplish, in connection with slavery, we cannot know; but, whilst we deplore existing evils, and do what we can scripturally to remove them, let us not forget, that God is glorified in bringing good out of evil— great good out of great evil—making "the wrath of man to praise him, and restraining the remainder thereof." The people of God may not become impatient, because the results from their legitimate labors are not such as they desired or expected, and attempt to take the Providence of God out of His hands by seizing the sword, and removing wrongs or evils by violence.

Just here we see one of the great errors of Abolitionists. Judging from any of those writings that I have seen, one would never imagine—that they acknowledge Divine providence in this thing. It seems never to have occurred to them—that God may have great purposes yet to be accomplished by means of it; and that they cannot defeat those purposes. Let us not forget the *wheel within a wheel.*

Before proceeding with the discussion, I propose to state several points in relation to which, I presume, we are nearly or quite unanimous. Much is gained, in controversial discussions, by ascertaining how far the parties agree, and where they differ.

1. We agree, that slavery will terminate. It was not in the beginning; and it will not be at the end. It originated in sin, degradation and violence; and the grace and the providence of God will ultimately remove the effects of sin. It will not exist in the Millenial day; and unless that day shall speedily dawn, we hope for its disappearance sooner.

2. We agree, that it must have either a peaceful or a bloody end. If bloody, then must the great mass of the slaves perish in the conflict. This is inevitable.

3. If it is to have a peaceful end, it must end with the consent and by the action of those who have it to deal with. On this point there can be no dispute.

4. If it is to end with their consent and by their action; they must be influenced either by their worldly interests, or by moral principle, or by both. Slave labor may become unprofitable. Or moral principle may become strong enough and prevalent enough to overcome mere selfish considerations. Or both interest and moral principle may combine to produce the result.

5. Unless providential events and moral influences shall, to a very extraordinary extent, change the ordinary course of things, emancipation must be *gradual*, and in connection with *colonization*. The feeling which prevails in both the slaveholding and the free States, forbids the reasonable expectation, that the nearly four millions of slaves will be suddenly emancipated on the soil. In the West India Islands, emancipation may be said to have been immediate; but the British parliament had the constitutional power to abolish slavery; and the government paid the owners for their slaves. In our country, there is no constitutional power outside of the States where it exists, that can interfere with it. If the emancipation shall occur, it must be under the gradual change of public sentiment in the slave States; and time will be required to effect such a change. And beyond a doubt, this must take place in connection with colonization—the removal of the blacks to some other place.

7. Christians can desire and seek only a peaceful termination of it. "The Prince of Peace" has given them "the sword of the Spirit," and has bidden them fight with it. He has no more authorized us to march into the slave States to liberate the slaves, than he authorized Peter the hermit and the Pope of Rome to

preach up the Crusades, in order to recover the Holy Land from
the possession of infidels. War, pestilence and famine are God's
judgments; neither of them has been intrusted to his Church
for the purpose of effecting reforms.

Until very recently, I should have expected a unanimous
agreement to the statement in regard to the peaceful termination
of slavery; but I have recently seen doctrines and principles
advocated by ministers of the Gospel, which seem to me to equal
the worst morality of the Koran. I am happy to say—the number
of those who have advanced such sentiments, is small.

8. If we cannot see how and when slavery is to end, it is
clearly the duty of Christians to bring to bear upon it such moral
influences, as will most effectually mitigate the evils of it, and
prepare for its removal, as soon as Divine providence shall
open the way.

9. The Gospel is the divinely appointed means for effecting all
moral reforms, for mitigating existing evils, and for preparing the
way for, and effecting salutary changes in society.

10. We are thus brought to the statement of a great principle,
which, if regarded, will aid us in reaching a safe conclusion
respecting the true method of treating slavery, viz: *In cases in
which we have to deal with particular sins or evils, with which
the Apostles of Christ had to deal, their teaching and example
must guide us; since they were guided by the Holy Spirit.* We
may not take the general principles of the Scriptures, and make
an application of them to any sin or evil, contrary to the
application of those principles, made by the Apostles to sins
or evils of the same character. Suppose we had a book, written
under the Divine guidance, in which the general principles of
medical science were stated and explained, and in which also the
treatment of a number of particular diseases by inspired physicians, was detailed. What would be thought of a physician, who
would attempt to apply the general principles stated, to the
treatment of a particular disease, without inquiring how the same
disease was treated by inspired physicians?

Were the Apostles called to deal with slavery? We agree, that
they were. Was the slavery with which they had to deal, identical, in its character, with that with which we have to deal? If
it was, how did they treat it? Having settled these questions,
we have inspired directions, how we should treat it. Abolitionists

affirm—that the slavery with which the Apostles had to deal, was identical with American slavery. "See," says Rev. J. Blanchard, "how perfectly the American and Roman slave systems coincide." "Such was Roman Slavery," says Dr. Thompson, "and this is the Slavery which, in its essential feature of chattelism, and with many of its horrid incidents, has been transmitted to our times, and exists upon our soil." "And this," says another writer, "is Slavery everywhere."

Since, then, it is not only admitted, but asserted, that the slavery with which the Apostles had to deal, is identical with that with which we are concerned; it is a question of peculiar importance—*How did they treat it?* Beyond a doubt, their desire was not only to reform sinners, but to elevate and bless the degraded and oppressed. In their methods of effecting these objects, they were guided by the Holy Spirit; and their teaching and example are placed on record for the guidance of the ministers and the Church of Christ in all ages. What were their methods?

In dealing with this evil, the Apostles were, in two respects, situated as we are, viz: 1st. They found slavery already in existence; and so did we. 2d. They could neither abolish slavery, or amend the laws regulating it, except as they could reach the governing mind with right moral influences; and neither can we. The Roman government was not controlled by God's law; neither are our Legislatures. We call ourselves a Christian people; but who goes to one of our Legislatures, or to the majority of the people, to find a supreme regard for the Scriptures? The Apostles might have modified the laws by reaching *one mind*; we are obliged to reach the multitude, and to mould public sentiment, against strong prejudices and large pecuniary interests.

I propose now to test the question, whether the mode of dealing with slavery, adopted by the Presbyterian Church and by others agreeing with us, is the true one, for most effectively mitigating its evils, and most safely and speedily abolishing it; or whether the mode adopted by the Abolitionists is the true one. Let us test it in two ways, viz:

1. By enquiring into the Apostolic mode of treating it.
2. By comparing the results of the different modes.

I. The Apostolic mode of treating slavery, embraced two particulars, viz:

1. In the first place, their plan was to preach the Gospel—the whole Gospel—to masters and slaves. Examine all their discourses and parts of discourses recorded in the Acts of the Apostles; and you will find ample proof of this statement. Paul tells us distinctly *how* he preached, and *why* he preached thus. "We preach Christ crucified." Why? Because such preaching is "the power of God and the wisdom of God "— Divine wisdom and Divine power combined to turn men from all sin. This is what we need. So clear was the Apostle, that this was the true way, that he determined not to know any thing else among the people. 1 Cor. 1 : 18 and 2 : 2.

So far as the masters were concerned, the Apostles secured three results, viz : 1st. They saved their souls, to the glory of the Redeemer. 2d. They established the authority of God in their hearts, and awakened in them the earnest desire to know and to do their whole duty—their duty to their servants, as well as to others. This was a great gain. Every true convert became a *disciple ;* and his first question was : "Lord, what wilt thou have me to do?" Then it was comparatively easy to teach them their duty. They would hear and heed. 3d. They secured the influence of their example over others—thus forming a purer public sentiment—"That ye may be blameless and harmless, the sons of God without rebuke, in the midst of a crooked and perverse nation, among whom ye shine as lights in the world, holding forth the word of life." This was the leaven, destined to leaven the whole lump—to remove sin and its evils.

Thus *war* is to terminate, and slavery with it—not by peace societies, but by the diffusion of the doctrines and truths of the Gospel. Isaiah, 2 : 3, 4. Swords will be converted to ploughshares, and spears to pruning-hooks, just as soon as the Gospel shall rule among the nations ; and the same spirit which puts an end to war, will forever abolish slavery—one of the fruits of war.

So far as the slaves were concerned, the Apostles accomplished several objects, viz :

They secured to them the highest freedom—their emancipation from the thraldom of sin, and the slavery of the devil. So far is this freedom superior to the other, that Paul said to converted slaves : "Care not for it : for he that is called in the Lord, being a servant, is the Lord's freeman." And now let me propound two or three questions to our Abolitionist friends :—

Which is more important to the slaves, emancipation from the slavery of sin and the devil, or emancipation from the control of earthly masters? If we can secure but one of these blessings for them, which is it most important to secure? In eternity for whose influence will the converted slaves feel most thankful to God—that of the men who clamored for their temporal freedom, neglecting their eternal interests, or that of those who went amongst them and labored for their spiritual deliverance? There can be but one answer.

Again: For which of these things did our Saviour die, and which has he specially commanded us to seek? Great as is the blessing of freedom, we are not taught that our Lord died to secure it to men, but to "save his people from their sins." And the commission he placed in the hands of his ministers and people, is to preach his Gospel "to every creature." If freedom to all results from the preaching of the Gospel, as it will, it is well; but we may not turn aside from our great work and from the great object to secure one infinitely inferior.

I cannot help contrasting the course pursued by our Abolition friends, with that of the Moravian Christians, whose praise is in all the churches. They saw the slaves in the West India Islands, in ignorance and sin; and such was their desire for their conversion to God, that some of them offered to sell themselves into slavery, in order to preach the glorious Gospel to them. This has been regarded a most wonderful manifestation of Christian affection. But now you hear Christian men all over the land clamoring about their emancipation, but manifesting little concern for their souls. And what is certainly remarkable, they are preaching vociferously, from Sabbath to Sabbath, on this subject, to those who are of the same opinion with themselves, but who can do nothing to effect the desired object!

2. If the Apostles did not secure freedom to the slaves, they did greatly mitigate the evils of their servitude, and secure for them that which made them happy in spite of slavery. They mitigated the evils of slavery; for every master brought under the influence of the Gospel, became a better master. No matter whether the slave code of Rome was improved or not, he governed his family and his servants according to the word of God; so that wherever the Gospel was preached, masters became humane and regardful of the interests of their servants, looking upon them as their fellow men, whose happiness they were bound

to promote. Thus by the influence of the Gospel pressing the truth upon hearts and consciences of masters, the Apostles lifted the pressure from off the slaves; and their condition became comparatively happy.

Moreover, the Apostles were instrumental in securing that which made them happy in spite of slavery. It is a blessed truth, that the grace of God can make all who are its subjects happy, in spite of outward circumstances. The Kingdom of God is in its nature "righteousness, and peace, and joy in the Holy Ghost." Paul and Silas, scourged and cast into prison, with their feet made fast in the stocks, at the hour of midnight, prayed and sang praises to God. So may all the disciples of Christ, bond and free, sing—

"And prisons would palaces prove,
    If Jesus would dwell with me there."

Abolitionists may say—slaveholders will not let us go and preach among them. How do you account for it, that, under a system of unmitigated slavery, the Apostles of Christ could preach to masters and slaves, declaring "the whole counsel of God," whilst our Abolition friends cannot do the same thing in our country? The Apostles frequently encountered mobs, but you read of not a single mob excited by their preaching against slavery? How shall we account for the singular fact, that the Apostles could so preach against slavery in the Roman Empire, as to mitigate all its evils, and melt it away, whilst Abolitionists everywhere stir up the worst passions, and defeat their own aims? Their preaching must differ very widely from that of the Apostles on the same subject.

II. The second particular in the Apostolic mode of dealing with slavery, was, their receiving into the churches both masters and slaves, so far as they gave evidence of conversion, and prescribing the relative duties of each. Thus they brought masters and slaves under the influence of the Gospel, and under the supervision of the church, and together they were accustomed to partake of their Saviour's body and blood. The instructions of the Apostles to both masters and slaves, are worthy of special attention; and they stand in strong contrast with those of many modern ministers. Fidelity on the part of servants was enjoined as their *religious duty*—as service rendered to their Saviour. "Servants," said Paul, "be obedient to them that are your masters according to the flesh, with fear and trembling, in singleness of your heart, as unto Christ, not with eye service, as man pleasers; but as the servants of Christ, doing the will of God from the heart; with good will doing service, as to the Lord, and not to men "—Eph. 6 : 5, 7. And they were commanded to count their masters worthy of all honor, " that the name of God and his doctrine be not blasphemed "—1 Tim. 6 : 1, 2. If Christian servants should be unfaithful or disobedient to their masters, the name of God would be dishonored, as it is now through the influence of ministers who seem to regard themselves as wiser than the Apostles.

Masters, too, were required to discharge their duties to their servants, as in the sight of God, who would hold them accountable. "Masters, do the same things unto them, forbearing threatening, knowing that your Master also is in Heaven ; neither is there respect of persons with him." " Masters give unto your servants that which is just and equal : knowing that ye have a Master in Heaven." Thus, instead of the civil code of Rome, the Gospel of Christ was to control the conduct of both master and servant—making both faithful in the discharge of their relative duties. " He taught them," says Rev. A. Barnes, " their duty towards those who were under them, and laid down principles, which, if followed, would lead ultimately to universal freedom. * * * * If the master and his slave were both Christians, even if the relation continued, it would be a relation of mutual confidence. The master would become the protector, the teacher, the guide, the friend ; the servant would become the faithful helper—rendering service to one whom he loved, and to whom he felt himself bound by the obligations of gratitude and affection."

By this mode of treating slavery, the Apostles accomplished two objects, viz. : they mitigated and almost annihilated the evils of slavery ; and they secured its ultimate abolition. " By ignoring the Roman law of slavery, and placing both master and servant under the higher law of Christian love and equality—the Apostles decreed the virtual abolition of slavery, and did in time subdue it, wherever Christianity gained the ascendancy in society or in the State."—Dr. Thompson.

This teaching of the Apostles, as most Abolitionists admit and assert, was, in its character and tendencies, decidedly anti-

slavery. Now, it is a fact, which cannot be disputed, that the
teaching and the course of the Presbyterian Church are precisely the same. Why, then, is she denounced as *pro-slavery*,
whilst they are declared to have been *anti-slavery?* How can it
be, that the same teaching and the same course which abolished
slavery *then*, perpetuates it *now?* Who will undertake to answer
these questions? And since Abolitionists insist, that the Apostles,
by their instruction and methods of proceeding, *virtually* abolished
slavery, and finally secured its entire removal, why have they not
been content to follow their example? Are they wiser or more
faithful?

The truth, I fear, is—that many professing Christians, and
even ministers, have so much confidence in their own wisdom,
that the Scriptures are of little authority with them. Very
recently, a Congregational Association in Connecticut licensed
some four young men to preach the Gospel, not one of whom
professed to believe the whole Bible inspired. The disposition
to trample under foot the Word of God, seems rapidly increasing,
even in the church! We must be excused for still sitting at the
feet of the Great Teacher.

2. I now propose to test the merits of the two modes of treating slavery, by their respective fruits. This is a Scriptural and
safe test—"By their fruits ye shall know them." The true
character of professed ministers of Christ and the truth of their
doctrines are infallibly indicated by their effects. I am willing to
have our views and our method of dealing with slavery tested in
this way. Facts will show who are *pro*-slavery, and who *anti*-
slavery.

1. It is a fact, that the method of treating slavery, which we
have adopted, abolished it in the Roman Empire. Its evils were
gradually mitigated, until it entirely disappeared. It is a fact,
worthy to be remembered, that in the primitive church, and in
the church through succeeding ages, the mere holding of slaves
was never, to any extent, made a bar to Christian fellowship.
No one, so far as I know, pretends to prove that it was. Nevertheless, it may be well to adduce some testimony.

When the Abolitionists were pressing their doctrines upon the
Free Church of Scotland, insisting on excluding from Christian
fellowship all slaveholders, Dr. Chalmers said—"We hope that
our Free Church will never deviate to the right or the left
from the path of undoubted principle. But we hope, on the

other hand, that she will not be frightened from her propriety, or forced by clamor of any sort to outrun her own convictions, so as to adopt, at the bidding of other parties, a new and factitious principle of administration, for which she can see no authority in Scripture, and of which she can gather no traces in the history or practice of the churches in Apostolic times." Not only did not this doctrine prevail in the Apostolic churches; but Dr. Chalmers could find no trace of it. The testimony of the very learned church historian, NEANDER, is in point. He says: "Christianity brought about that change in the consciousness of humanity, from which a dissolution of this whole relation, though it could not be immediately effected, yet, by virtue of the consequences resulting in that change, must eventually take place. This effect Christianity produced, first, by the facts of which it was a witness; and next by the ideas which by occasion of these facts it set in circulation. Servants and masters, if they had become believers, were brought together under the same bond of heavenly union, destined for immortality; they became brethren in Christ, in whom is neither bond nor free. * * * Masters looked upon their servants no longer as slaves, but as their beloved brethren; they prayed and sang in company: they could sit at each other's side at the feast of brotherly love, and receive together the body of the Lord. Thus, by the spirit and by the effects of Christianity, ideas and feelings could not fail of being diffused, which were directly opposed to this relation, so consonant to the habits of thinking that had hitherto prevailed. * * * * * * Yet Christianity never began with outward revolutions and changes, which in all cases where they have not been prepared within, and are not based upon conviction, fail of their salutary ends. It gave servants first, the true inward freedom, without which the outward and earthly freedom is a mere show.

Dr. Charles Hase, Professor of Theology, of Jena, says: "The church has always endeavored to mitigate the evils of slavery"—he does not assert that it made it a term of communion,—" and as soon as she possessed of the power, to restrain them by legal enactments. But it was not until sometime in the middle ages that the last remnants of European slavery were abolished by law."

The testimony of both these learned historians establishes the truth, that slavery was abolished in the Roman empire, not by excluding all slaveholders from the Church of Christ, nor by denouncing them as heinous sinners, but by the gradual diffusion of the doctrines and principles of the Gospel. The Gospel was preached to masters and slaves; and both entered the church together; and as the warmth of the sun gradually melts away the snow, and ice, and frosts of winter, so did Christianity melt away slavery. Time was required to effect the result; but it was attained. Beyond a question, it is true that the method of treating slavery, which we have adopted, did first mitigate, and remove its evils, and finally abolish it in the Roman empire.

2. Our method of dealing with slavery abolished it in every one of the States of this Union, in which it has been abolished. It has not been a great while, since slavery existed extensively in New England, and also in New York, New Jersey and Pennsylvania. How was it abolished in those States? Not by denouncing slaveholders as criminals, and excluding them from the churches, but by the gradual and silent operation of the principles of the Gospel.

I have before stated, and I now repeat, that in none of the leading churches or denominations of these States was slaveholding ever made, to any extent, a matter of ecclesiastical discipline. It is impossible to find a trace of anything of the sort, except in a very few of the churches. How, then, came it to be abolished in New England, New York, Pennsylvania and New Jersey?

The venerable Dr. Spring, himself the son of a Congregational minister, now some seventy-five years of age, and who ought to be familiar with this subject, tells us how it was abolished. He says: "Where the Bible has begun to exert its influence, it gradually remedies the evil and wears it away. It did it in Massachusetts. * * * It did it in Connecticut, and statutes were passed in 1783 and 1797, which have, in their gentle and gradual operation, totally extinguished slavery in that State. It did it in New Jersey. It did it Pennsylvania." In New York, where the slave laws were very severe, he remarks: "In process of time the penal code against slaves was meliorated; facilities were multiplied for the manumission of slaves, and the importation of slaves was at length prohibited. Laws were enacted also, to teach the slaves to read, and a system commenced for the gradual abolition of slavery. * * * Is it not true that the Bible has silently and gradually, so meliorated the relation between the master and the slave, that in the progress of its principles and spirit, it must ultimately, either abolish the relation, or leave it on a basis of the purest benevolence?"

No doubt, the comparatively small number of slaves in these States, and the greater value of the labor of white men, had their influence in removing slavery; and no doubt, many sold their slaves to the South, instead of emancipating them. But so far as emancipation was the result of religious influence and moral principle, that influence was diffused by the preaching of the Gospel to masters and slaves. We find no exciting debates in ecclesiastical bodies in relation to the excommunication of slaveholders as such, and no violent denunciations of them in the publications of that period. The work progressed silently and gradually, till public sentiment moulded the legislation of the several States, and led to plans of gradual emancipation.

3. Our method of treating slavery emancipated large numbers in the slaveholding States, before recent agitation led to the enactment of laws prohibiting emancipation without removal. Rev. Dr. Baird, whose accuracy in statistical statements will not be questioned, stated, in his account of the state and prospects of religion in America, made to the Evangelical Alliance in Paris, that in 1850, there were in Virginia 54,332 free colored people; in Maryland, 74,723; in all the slave States, 290,424; and he remarks: "These people, or their ancestors obtained their freedom by the influence of the Gospel on the hearts of their former masters." Here are nearly half a million in the slaveholding States, who obtained their freedom—how? Not by the teaching of Abolitionists, but by our mode of treating slavery. The Gospel was faithfully preached to masters and slaves, and their relative duties pressed upon them.

If you will take the trouble to look over the Minutes of the old Synod of Virginia, you will find the members of their churches repeatedly exhorted to educate their slaves, and thus prepare them for emancipation. The same is true of the Synod of Kentucky. In the free States, we learn from Dr. Baird, there were 204,484 free colored people, a large portion of whom were emancipated in the same way. Let the candid hearer, in view of such facts, judge whether the doctrines we preach and the course we advocate, do or do not promote emancipation.

4. The mode of treating slavery, which we advocate, was in successful operation—multiplying the number of emancipated

slaves, when modern Abolitionism arose to defeat it. I think it
proper to call special attention to the fact, that when it arose, it
did not find the churches and the country asleep on this subject.
The condition of the slaves, and the best and most expeditious
method of securing to them freedom and prosperity, had long
engaged, and were then enlisting the earnest inquiries of Christians and philanthropists, both in the North and in the South.
Soon after our country secured its independence, general attention
was turned to the subject. Dr. Alexander says, "The condition
of the slaves occupied the attention of many serious, sagacious
men in Virginia, about the close of the last century. It was
often the subject of free conversation among enlightened men,
and their opinions generally were favorable to the emancipation
of the slaves, both on principles of justice and sound policy."
Such continued to be the prevailing feeling up to 1832, when the
subject was earnestly discussed by political men.

In the *Christian Observer*, published in Boston, in 1816, I
find a letter from a gentleman in Maryland, containing the
following interesting statements:

"*Now* emancipation (in Maryland) seems to engage the attention of all ranks. Societies are forming in most of the slave
States, in some instances almost exclusively by slaveholders, for
the express purpose of promoting that interesting measure.
Formerly, the *right* to hold slaves was scarcely ever questioned;
now, it is admitted on all sides, that they are justly entitled to
their liberty. Under this impression, many are disposed to
emancipate them, but are not willing to turn them loose without
education upon the community. To a petition circulated by the
Abolition Society of Tennessee to the Legislature of that State,
for some legislative provision in the case, there were upwards of
1500 signatures; and as an evidence of their earnest desire for
the consummation of their request, many of the slaveholders
were so particular as to write opposite their names—"Slaveholder."—In this State (Maryland) emancipation seems to be the
order of the day. Many families of the first rank have recently
manumitted their slaves. Few die now without making provision
for their enlargement; and I trust that the time is near at hand,
when the Legislature will pass an act to register and secure the
freedom of such as may be born hereafter."

In Kentucky, not only the Church, but leading politicians were exerting their influence in favor of a plan of gradual emancipation. With a view to this, a law was passed, forbidding any one to import slaves into the State, unless he would state under oath that they were for his own use, not for sale. In 1830, there was an Abolitionist Society in Kentucky—not of the modern type, but a society of emancipationists, as were those in Tennessee.

In those days, the subject of slavery was freely discussed. I sat in the Synod of Kentucky, and heard the whole subject earnestly discussed, and a plan of emancipation earnestly recommended. In all the slaveholding˜States, under the influence of the Gospel, there was a growing sentiment in favor of emancipation.

Now, there might have been some excuse for the course of modern Abolitionists, if they had found the country and the churches either advocating slavery, or indifferent to its evils, and to the rights of slaves. But the state of things was widely different. By the diffusion of Christian principles, perhaps mainly, slavery had been banished from a number of the States; and under the operation of the same principles, the work of emancipation was moving forward with increasing rapidity. When Lafayette visited this country, he expressed the confident opinion, that within fifty years, Maryland, Virginia and Kentucky would be added to the list of free States; and his opinion was well grounded. But in an evil hour, Abolitionism was born. Its first note was one of discord, and its first effect to stop the progress of the great work.

5. Our method of dealing with slavery, originated, and has sustained the Colonization Society, of which Henry Clay said: "We may boldly challenge the annals of human nature for the record of any plan for the amelioration of the condition or advancement of the happiness of our race, which promised more unmixed good, or more comprehensive beneficence, than that of African Colonization, if carried into full execution." I subscribe most heartily to the sentiment.

This noble society was organized at Washington City in 1817; and many of the most prominent men in the nation were its patrons. The General Assembly of the Presbyterian Church was prompt to throw the weight of its influence in favor of the enterprise. That body, in 1818, said: "We recommend to all our people to patronize and encourage the Society lately formed for colonizing in Africa, the land of their ancestors, the free people of color in our country. We hope that much good may result from the plans and efforts of this Society. And while we exceedingly rejoice to have witnessed its organization among the *holders of slaves*, as giving an unequivocal pledge of their desire to deliver themselves and their country from this calamity of slavery, we hope that those portions of the American Union whose inhabitants are, by a gracious Providence, more favorably circumstanced, will cordially, and liberally, and earnestly co-operate with their brethren in bringing about the great end contemplated." Similar resolutions were adopted by many succeeding Assemblies.

Whilst the immediate design of the Society was to colonize, with their own consent, in Africa, the free people of color, or those who might be emancipated; it was also designed to break up the infamous slave-trade, and to send the Gospel and a Christian colonization to Africa. But its friends had still another object in view—one especially mentioned by the Assembly of 1818, viz: The promotion of the emancipation of the slaves. Dr. Alexander says: "It was believed by the founders and advocates of this Society, that it would exercise a gradual and powerful influence on slavery, simply by furnishing benevolent and conscientious persons with an opportunity of emancipating their slaves, to their own advantage; and without injury to the country. There can be no doubt, that the great men whose names have been mentioned, patronized the Colonization Society especially in the hope, that gradually, but rapidly, it would tend to deliver the country from the incubus of slavery, in a way to which no one could have any right or reason to object."

Dr. Alexander further says—" There are thousands of slave-holders who would give up their slaves, if they were satisfied that Liberia would be a permanently safe and comfortable abode for them. The attention of many people of the South is now directed intensely towards this rising colony; and more, many are now educating their younger slaves with some view to their future residence in that land of promise."

His testimony respecting its results, as to emancipation, is equally clear and instructive. "The Colonization Society," says he, " while it never proposed emancipation as its object, has done more incidentally to promote emancipation, than all the Abolition societies in the country. Indeed, these have, so far as is known to us, redeemed no slaves from bondage, but without intending it, have, by the course which they have pursued, riveted the chains which confine the slaves more closely than ever."

The organization of this Society was hailed with delight by all the leading churches in the country, and was earnestly recommended by them all. The Legislatures of some twelve of the States, North and South, also endorsed it; and the Legislature of Maryland, in 1833, made an appropriation of two hundred thousand dollars towards the removal to Africa of such people of color, as might be willing to emigrate. That Legislature, in recommending the Society, said—"As philanthropists and lovers of freedom, we deplore the existence of slavery among us, and would use our utmost exertions to ameliorate its condition." Indeed, there seemed a fair prospect, that Congress would take hold of the colonization cause, and push forward its noble plans.

Such was the state of things, and such the prospects of emancipation, when modern Abolitionism was born. Those called Abolitionists doubtless differ from each other, not only on other subjects connected with morals and religion, but respecting the extent to which it is proposed to go in opposition to slavery. The following doctrines, however, have been taught, with great earnestness, by men of respectable standing amongst them:

1. That slaveholding is sin in itself—"the sum of all villainies;" and, therefore, all slaveholders are to be denied Christian fellowship. Some only go so far as to assert, that the fact that a man is found holding a slave, is *prima facie* evidence of sin, and puts him upon the proof of his innocence.

2. That it is not only the right, but the duty of slaves to escape from their masters, if they can. Rev. Jas. Duncan, in his book republished by the Cincinnati Anti-Slavery Society, in 1840, says: "It appears self-evident that they are not only in duty bound to embrace the first favorable opportunity to escape from their tyrants, but it would be criminal to neglect it, so that no jury could decide such a case against the slave, without contracting great guilt and incurring damnation."

Gerrit Smith, who, I believe, has always stood well with Abolitionists, long before he avowed himself an infidel, gave to slaves the following advice: "And when, too, you are escaping from the matchless, horrible Bastile, take, all along your route, in the free as well as in the slave States, so far as it is absolutely essential to your escape, the horse, the boat, the food, the clothing which you may require; and feel no more compunction for the justifiable appropriation, than does the drowning man for possessing himself of the plank that floats in his way." He afterwards said—"The address has developed the devilism of the clerical toads, and other toads, among us."

3. The right and the duty to excite slaves to run from their masters, and to aid them in their flight. We have all heard of "the underground railroad," and it is set off attractively in "Uncle Tom's Cabin."

4. The right of slaves to kill their masters in order to gain their freedom. Mr. Duncan's book already quoted, maintains, that to aid in suppressing a slave insurrection, would be a damning sin. Joshua Leavit, whilst editing the *Emancipator*, said, humane men were thinking of reasoning with slaveholders with "cold steel." The *Independent* advised fugitive slaves to kill those who would arrest them. "If you die thus," says the editors, "you die nobly, and your blood shall be the redemption of your race." The same paper advised them to form a secret society with pass words, one of whose objects should be that of "spreading information among the slaves of the South as to the means and methods of escape."

Such are the doctrines which have been taught by men prominent in the ranks of Abolitionists, for quarter of a century. Doubtless there are many Abolitionists who would not adopt all of them; but if they have met with any rebuke from that quarter, I have not seen it. It is an astounding fact, that ministers of Christ are found, in our country, not only justifying, but applauding the morality of the Harper's Ferry invasion. The *Congregational Herald*, of this city, proclaimed John Brown a Christian martyr; and the *Covenanter*, of Philadelphia, does substantially the same thing. I had remarked, in the *Expositor*, that, if the teaching of Abolitionists is true, the only error of Brown consisted in moving without reasonable prospect of success. The *Covenanter* answers—"Amen, we say with all seriousness and earnestness. It is an evidence of the degeneracy of our age and of our land, that there are not thousands actuated by the spirit of John Brown in his quenchless hostility to slavery. But the right is progressing, and John Brown's heroic, and not fruitless devotion of himself to liberty, will prove like oil on the smoking embers of the fire of liberty. * * * Future ages will assign him a niche of glory in the records of earth," &c.

This statement of the principles of Abolitionism is sufficient to show what must have been, and must ever be their effects. But let us inquire for *facts*. The doctrines have borne abundant fruits; and those fruits are the infallible index to their true character.

1. Abolitionism has been zealously propagating its doctrines, and urging its practices, for about thirty years; and not a single slave State has been added to the list of free States; nor has it effected any improvement in the laws of any one State. Rev. Dr. Kirk, of Boston—an ardent anti-slavery man, a few years ago, said publicly—"For thirty years, hard words, and some very ugly ones have been used; and if any good has been accomplished, it is very slow; for not a single statute in any slave State has been altered or repealed." With such results, is it not time for the Abolitionists to pause, and inquire whether they have not greatly erred in their mode of treating Slavery?

2. How many slaveholders have they prevailed on to emancipate their slaves? Probably not one. It is said, and it is doubtless true, that by secret plans and emissaries some slaves have been induced to run from their masters, and have been helped on to Canada. So far as I am informed, we have no report of their success in this department of labor. It is very certain, however, that the number of slaves actually freed by them is very small.

3. Having accomplished little or nothing towards securing the freedom of the slaves, Abolitionists have done the cause of emancipation infinite injury, by their violent opposition to the cause of African Colonization. So prosperous was this cause in 1832, that Dr. Alexander says—"At one time, it seemed as if the expression of opinion in the Legislatures of the States, in the ecclesiastical bodies of all denominations, and in the meetings of the people, would have so pressed this subject on the attention of Congress, that, in obedience to the voice of the people, the national government would have not only patronized the Society, but have extended over Liberia, the broad shield of its protection."

Who was it that blasted these fair prospects? "It was," says Dr. Alexander, "during this year (1832) of general prosperity in the affairs of the Colonization Society, that a spirit of unrelenting opposition to the cause, arose from the friends of immediate emancipation, many of whom had been once favorers of Colonization. * * * The leader in this hostile attack, was Mr. Garrison, who published a large book against African Colonization.

Of this work, the editor of a paper in the city of New York, says—"The boldness, the magnitude, and the severity of his charges against the Society are truly astonishing.' This work seemed at once to arouse the feelings of many persons, who with zeal embraced Mr. Garrison's views; among these were found ministers of the gospel, and men and women of irreproachable character. This was the origin of what is now called Abolitionism. * * * Mr. Garrison's zeal was not satisfied by his written publications in this country, but as Mr. Cresson was in England, and successfully winning favor to the cause there, Mr. Garrison determined to follow him, and counteract his influence, by presenting his own views."

The zeal of Abolitionists waxed warmer and warmer against the colonization cause. James G. Birney and Gerrit Smith, once ardent and efficient friends of the cause, went over to the Abolitionists, and became no less zealous in defeating its plans. In the free States, and especially in New England, the Society was almost abandoned; and it narrowly escaped bankruptcy and ruin. "The enemies of the Colonization Society were not contented to confine themselves to argument and declamation, against the principles of the society, but they industriously and insidiously attempted to bring the colony into disrepute, by having recourse to slander and misrepresentation."—*Alexander.*

The Republic of Liberia now stands before the world, the triumphant vindication of the Presbyterian Church, and of her mode of treating slavery, and as a withering rebuke of the errors and wrong doings of Abolitionism. For, although the Presbyterian Church did not originate the colonization enterprise, (it did not fall within the range of her work,) it was the result of that mode of treating slavery, which she has adopted; and from the beginning, it had the weight of her influence.

Though late, some of the Abolitionists have been compelled to see, that this enterprize is a glorious one. The last thing we saw from the pen of James G. Birney, was his advice to the colored people to go to Liberia, in which he expressed his conviction, that the colonization cause was of God. And the Congregationalist of Boston, in spite of its Abolitionism, bears the following testimony:

"*American Colonization Society.* It claims to have established a colony in Africa, that has already been acknowledged an Independent Republic by the principal governments in the world—to have settled Christianity on a permanent footing, preparing the principal agency for sending it abroad over the whole dark and populous continent—to have planted there American civilization, giving the people a constitution like our own—laws, schools, arts, language and newspapers, besides rearing a college edifice, and supporting a public library of great value—and to have furnished thousands of free people of color with a home, where they labor under none of the disadvantages of an inferior caste; where hope animates them to noble exertions, and they may fairly aspire to all offices of trust and honor, even to the Presidency. The march of the Republic is onward—men who, but a few years ago were slaves in Virginia and Kentucky, now own farms and large plantations of coffee, sugar, and other valuable productions. Commerce, too, increases, as the immense internal resources of the country are brought to light, and colored men, in a few years, amass handsome fortunes ; and educational systems are becoming perfected—schools and seminaries are springing up in every direction—so that the next generation of Liberia will possess a sound, classical, religious education ; and besides all this the moral atmosphere is healthful—the Sabbath is reverenced along the coast and in the interior, and by those who come from a distance to Liberia for purposes of trade. Thus much is gained.''

Yes—thus much is gained, in spite of the early, long-continued, unmitigated opposition of Abolitionists. And ten times as much might have been gained, both for the slaves and for Africa, if Abolitionism had never been born. In its advocates, the cause of colonization and of emancipation has encountered its chief difficulties. Abolitionists of the North, and pro-slavery men of the South, however they differed in other things, agreed in opposing this cause.

Now, let the fact be remembered—that Abolitionism arose under the lead of a bad man, who has long been a blaspheming infidel, and its first, its most zealous work, for many years, was violent opposition to the noblest work of the nineteenth century. Yea, and its chief weapons were misrepresentation and slander ; for now it is demonstrated, so as to silence the bitterest enemy, that its charges against the colonization society were false. Claiming to be the special friends of the slaves and of emancipation, Abo-

litionists threw their whole weight against the great emancipation
society, which commanded the confidence, and enlisted the energies
of all denominations of Christians, of large numbers of men not
professors of religion, and of many Legislatures! The agents
of this society found no difficulty in exposing the great evils of
slavery, and of pleading the cause of emancipation; for they
offered to remove from the country the emancipated slaves, and
place them where they would be truly free. One of the most
powerful emancipation speeches I ever read, was made by Henry
Clay, at the anniversary of a Colonization Society. By the
truths thus put forth, public sentiment was rapidly undergoing a
change in favor of emancipation. But Abolitionists denounced
the society and all connected with it as *pro-slavery*, just as they
now denounce and misrepresent every man who will not adopt
their opinions.

Now, I ask—did ever any good thing have such an origin, as
Abolitionism had?—under the lead of a bad man, bitterly opposing the noblest enterprize, and opposing it by misrepresentation and slander? Is it not time for Abolitionists to stop their
denunciations of those who have steadfastly sustained colonization and emancipation, long enough to give some plausible reason
for the course they have pursued toward this noble cause? If,
as is certain, the Colonization Society has really secured the
emancipation of more slaves, than all the Abolitionists in the
land; it is a fair question, which most deserves the name of
pro-slavery—the Presbyterians who sustained the society, or the
Abolitionists, who did everything in their power to destroy it?

4. Abolitionism has divided the friends of emancipation, and
broken the moral power, that was effectually operating for the
removal of slavery from the country. Does any man believe,
that Elliot Cresson, the noble-hearted philanthropist, was a
pro-slavery man? Yet Garrison, who claimed to be ardently
opposed to slavery, expended his time and energies in destroying
the influence of Cresson. And so it has been in every part of
the land, for a quarter of a century. Tens of thousands of men,
equally anxious for the abolition of slavery, have been arraigned
against each other, whilst the evil has rapidly gained strength.

How stands the matter now? The Congregational Associa-
tions of New England, twenty-five years ago, wielded a powerful
and happy influence in favor of emancipation. Now that influence is annihilated. They cannot exert one particle of influence

in favor of the slaves. Nay—every attempt to do any thing, simply produces greater exasperation. Twenty-five years ago, the Methodist Church exerted its unbroken influence in favor of emancipation. Now, divided North and South—the one division drifting to pro-slavery, and the other to Abolitionism, they exert not a particle of influence for emancipation. The Baptist denomination has its influence very much crippled in the same way; and the New School body, divided, and the two parts running to opposite extremes, is likewise shorn of its moral power for benefitting the slaves.

A similar change has taken place outside of the churches. Formerly the people of the North and the South, and the Northern and Southern Legislatures were united in the noble effort to remove the curse of slavery from the country. Now they are divided in feeling, and opposed to each other in measures. The cause of these divisions is too well known. Abolitionism found the cause of emancipation going forward under the united influence of all denominations of Christians, and of the whole American people, with comparatively few exceptions. At the end of thirty years, it has broken and destroyed this mighty and happy influence; and what has it given us in its stead? Divisions, heart-burnings, hatred, variance, strife! Still, in the face of such facts, it shouts *pro-slavery* against every man who refuses to shut his eyes to all the past, and follow it.

5. Abolitionism has produced a terrible reaction against emancipation, and in favor of the perpetuity of slavery, in all the slaveholding States. The doctrines published by Abolitionists, and their modes of procedure, have produced the highest degree of irritation, which always drives men to extreme positions. Dr. Chalmers, judging from the character of these principles, declared his conviction, that such would be the result. He said: "There are various modes of procedure and policy, on which philanthropists and patriots might enter, and join their forces for the abolition of slavery. The most unjustifiable, and let me add, the most unwise and least effectual of all these, were to pronounce a wholesale anathema by which to unchristianize, or pass a general sentence of excommunication on slaveholders. But I must repeat my conviction, that slavery will not be at all shaken—it will be strengthened and stand its ground—if assailed through the medium of that most questionable and ambiguous

principle which the Abolitionists are now laboring to force upon
our acceptance, even that slaveholding is in itself, a ground of
exclusion from the Christian sacraments—instead of being assailed
through the medium of such other and obvious principles, as
come home to the hearts and consciences of all men."

As a matter of fact, this unhappy reaction is not only cotem-
porary with the rise of Abolitionism; but the effects of its
doctrines became immediately manifest, not only in Kentucky
and Virginia, where public sentiment was becoming increasingly
favorable to emancipation, but throughout the South. Dr.
Alexander, after mentioning the character of the publications
made, many of which tended strongly to excite the slaves to
insurrection, says: "Alarm and indignation spread through the
whole southern country. The effect on the people of the South,
in regard to slavery, was the very opposite of that aimed at;
and sentiments more favorable to the continuance and even
perpetuity of slavery, began now to be very commonly entertained; whereas before, such statements were scarcely ever
heard."

On this subject, Daniel Webster bore the following unequivocal testimony: "I cannot but see what mischief their interference
with the South has produced. And is it not plain to every man?
Let any gentleman who doubts that, recur to the debates in the
Virginia House of Delegates in 1832, and he will see with what
freedom a proposition made by Mr. Randolph for the gradual
abolition of slavery, was discussed in that body. Every one
spoke of slavery as he thought; very ignominious and disparag-
ing names and epithets were applied to it. The debates in the
House of Delegates on that occasion, I believe, were all published. They were read by every colored man who could read;
and if there were any who could not read, those debates were
read to them by others. At that time Virginia was not
unwilling nor afraid to discuss this question and to let that class
of her population know as much of it as they could learn. They
(the Abolitionists) attempted to arouse and did arouse a very
strong feeling; in other words they created great agitation in
the North against Southern slavery. Well, what was the result?
The bonds of the slave were bound more firmly, their rivets
more strongly fastened. Public opinion, which in Virginia had
begun to be exhibited against slavery, and was opening out for
the discussion of the question, drew back and shut itself up in

its castle. I wish to know whether anybody can now talk in Virginia, as Mr. Randolph, Gov. McDowell and others talked then openly, and sent their remarks to the press in 1832? We all know the fact, and we all know the cause; and everything that this agitating people have done, has been, not to enlarge, but to restrain; not to set free, but to bind faster the slave population of the South." Such is the testimony of Daniel Webster.

The venerable Dr. Spring, after mentioning the painful reaction in Kentucky and Virginia, says: "The late Dr. Griffin, one of the most devoted friends of the colored race in the land, said to me a few months before his death, "I do not see that the efforts in favor of immediate emancipation have effected anything, but to rivet the chains of the poor slave.'"

It is not difficult to see how this reaction was produced. The doctrines themselves were calculated to produce it—not only designing to exclude all slaveholders from the Church of Christ, but justifying, if not tending to excite slave insurrections. Then these doctrines, when first promulged, were taught by men in the free States, and were accompanied with the most offensive wholesale denunciations. Not only have we no scriptural authority for such a mode of procedure, but it has never been adopted with reference to any other evil or sin. Try the plan upon one of your neighbors, who, as you think, is living in sin. Collect several of your acquaintances, have addresses delivered, magnifying his criminality; pass offensive resolutions and publish them in the papers. Would any man in his senses expect to reform one of his neighbors in this way? Try the plan with the heathen. Let us have public meetings, and earnest and denunciatory addresses, setting forth, in strong light, the superstition and corruption of the Chinese. Send them to the emperor, along with your missionaries. Inform him of your purpose to rectify existing evils and improve his legislation. How will you succeed? Yet you will make such speeches, and publish such resolutions, and send them to the slave States—thus so exciting unconverted men, that nothing can be done to promote emancipation.

Connected with these doctrines, so unwisely promulged, was the sending of secret agents into the slave States, for the purpose of inducing slaves to leave their masters. To what extent Abolitionists have actually engaged in this business, I do not

pretend to know; but so far as I am informed, none of them
have condemned it. I myself knew an instance in which a minister, while attending the meetings of an ecclesiastical body, took
advantage of the hospitality of a gentleman who entertained him,
to interfere with his slaves. Who can wonder, that such doctrines
and practices have destroyed confidence, and rendered the
people of the South suspicious of those coming from the North?
The enactment of severe laws, the occurrence of mob violence,
and the like, date after the rise of Abolitionism. I cannot justify
these things. I could not justify a man for striking another for
an insult offered; but who that knows anything of human nature,
is surprised at it? Ministers of the Gospel and Christians are
inexcusable for pursuing a course to excite the evil passions of
men, when they are bound to try to reform them. They are the
less excusable, since, in relation to this very subject, they have
both the instruction, and the example of inspired men.

   6. Abolitionism has, as far as it could, taken the Gospel from
both masters and slaves—thus not only depriving the slaves of
the consolations and hopes of religion, but taking away the
Divinely appointed means of reforming sinners of all classes, and
of removing all kinds of evil. Our Congregational brethren
have missionaries in heathen lands; but they have none in the
slave States, about which, nevertheless, those of them who are
Abolitionists, have manifested so deep concern. Their sympa-
thies for the poor slaves have risen to the highest pitch; and
they have in their hands the most effectual of all agencies to
relieve them; but they have not used it! They have stood at a
distance and abused their masters, instead of carrying to them
the Gospel of Christ. The Home Missionary Society could
once sustain missionaries in the slave States; but Abolitionist
sympathy for the slave has rendered it impossible now; and
hence the formation of the Southern Aid Society, to enable
those who once sent their benefactions through the American
Home Missionary Society, to send the Gospel to the slave States.
The true spirit of Abolitionism was expressed by the *Congregationalist*, of Boston, some four years ago. "The destitutions in
Missouri," said the editors, "are great and lamentable; the vacant
churches are numerous, and withal feeble." "It is among the
last States of the Union in which any man of God can promise
himself usefulness or comfort." "Slavery is there in its worst
type and most revolting features." "If there be a single Lot in

such a Sodom, the voice from Heaven says to him—'Flee for thy life.'"

The plain English of this is—"The devil has taken possession of Missouri; let the soldiers of Christ run like cowards!" Apart from the fact that every one of these statements is untrue, what must we think of the sentiment? If slavery had been there in its most revolting forms—the slaves groaning under terrible oppression and cruelty—we would have supposed that Christians deeply sympathizing with them, would have hastened to carry the Gospel to masters and slaves, that its evils might be mitigated, and slavery abolished as soon as possible. Strange Christianity this! Did not slavery exist in the Roman Empire in its most revolting forms? Abolitionists agree with us that it did. Did the voice from Heaven, therefore, bid the Apostles flee for their lives? Did not that voice bid them go to master and slave, and preach to them "the unsearchable riches of Christ?" Whence, then, came the voice which the *Congregationalist* heard, bidding good men flee from Missouri, because slavery was there? Most assuredly it came not from Heaven. Yet, with few exceptions, Abolitionists have obeyed it, as if it had been the voice of God, for they have carefully avoided sending the Gospel to the slaveholding States.

7. Abolitionism has arrayed the great political parties against each other in a manner which threatens the ruin of the country. But for its agitations, there would have been no great zeal for extending slavery into new territories, nor any danger of its being extended. Politicians, North and South, are quick to see the hobbies on which they can ride into office and power. They have watched the increasing excitement and irritation upon the subject of slavery; and they have raised questions of the most threatening character upon it. It is a sad thing that the church and her ministry, whose office it is to subdue evil passions, and whose influence should bind the different parts of the country together, have been perverted, so as to excite the worst passions, and throw the tremendous influence of Christianity in favor of civil war with all its horrors.

The latest development of the doctrines of Abolitionism has been witnessed at Harper's Ferry. The chief actor in that scene did nothing more than to carry out in practice the doctrines of the book published, in 1840, by the Cincinnati Anti-Slavery Society, and of the *Independent* and the *Emancipator*. And now it is proclaimed by ministers of the Gospel *in this city* and elsewhere, that he is a Christian martyr, whose error was in the attempt to excite a slave insurrection, necessarily resulting in the most horrid scenes, *without reasonable prospect of success.* No Pope, in the dark ages, ever taught morality more corrupt and atrocious. There is nothing worse in Mahomet's Koran. According to this doctrine, Christian men may properly wait and pray for the day, when they may invade the slave States, and with fire and sword effect the emancipation of the slaves. I have hoped, that such doctrines are really held by very few; but when I see them taught without rebuke in a Denominational paper— the *Congregational Herald*, of this city, and in the *Covenanter*, of Philadelphia, I do not know how far they may have extended their influence.

And now, what are the results of thirty years of agitation? The progress of emancipation almost wholly stopped; constitutions and laws extensively adopted prohibiting emancipation without removal; the discussion of the evils of slavery in the slave States rendered impossible; an intense pro-slavery feeling pervading those States; the moral influence of the churches in favor of the slaves annihilated; the churches of all denominations divided and crippled; the North and the South arrayed in bitter hostility toward each other, with the dreadful prospect of civil war, and the ruin of this great nation, to the joy of despots in Europe, and the grief of all good men. Such are some, and only part, of the legitimate fruits of abolitionism; and the end is not yet.

I now close this discussion with a few remarks and suggestions.

I. The facts in the case show conclusively, which of the two modes of treating slavery is the scriptural and true one. "By their fruits ye shall know them." The mode which we insist upon has emancipated a thousand—I might say, ten thousand— slaves, where the Abolitionist mode has emancipated one. Our mode has greatly mitigated the evils of slavery, where it has not secured their emancipation; whilst every slave freed by the Abolitionist mode, has rendered the condition of hundreds of other slaves more hopeless and more miserable. Our mode has promoted emancipation, whilst it has promoted the spread of the Gospel, and built up the kingdom of Christ; whilst the Abolitionist mode has divided the Churches, and, to a great extent, destroyed their efficiency in the great work of evangelizing the world. The truth is, Abolitionism has abolished every good thing it has touched, and left slavery stronger than before. It is, in truth, a great *pro-slavery influence;* and southern pro-slavery men know that it is so. It affords them the opportunity to excite the people of the South, and urge them to make stronger the cords that bind the slaves.

As a Presbyterian, I am ready to compare notes with my Abolitionist friends. They denounce me and my Church as advocates of slavery. I am prepared to demonstrate, that we have emancipated a thousand slaves to their one, and that we have been instrumental in securing the *highest freedom* to a still greater number. The physicians who cure their patients, or improve their condition, are the true doctors. Others make a great ado, and publish their astonishing discoveries to the world; but the true test is the *cures effected.* I am prepared to stand the test. *Dare my Abolitionist friends do the same?* Abolitionism and steam doctoring belong to the same general class of remedies. Both kill a hundred, where they cure one.

II. Do you ask, what is our duty with regard to slavery? I answer—

1st. Preach the Gospel to masters and slaves. There are multitudes of faithful ministers in the slave States, who are preaching all that the Apostles ever preached on the subject; and no minister is authorized to preach anything more than they preached. Strangely enough, the day has come, when ministers of the Gospel are denounced, and that by Protestants, for not going further than the Bible, and preaching what is not in it. But if the Gospel is not faithfully preached in the slave States; send good men, who will preach it. But let those who are not disposed to go and preach the Gospel there, cease agitating, and leave the matter in the hands of those who are willing to undertake it. And if they will look around them, they will find enough to do in their own fields.

The Gospel is the great remedy for the evils of Society. Send it to the Slave States, and let it do its work.

2. Sustain the Colonization Cause. Abolitionists now begin to acknowledge indirectly their great error in so bitterly opposing it. When Paul was converted, he was as zealous in building up the Church, as he had been in pulling it down. Let Abolitionists imitate his example. But let them abandon the doctrines and

practices that have done so much mischief, and so little good.

Abolitionism and colonization will never work together. But the colonization cause presents a broad platform on which all friends of the slaves can stand, and work together. It has been tested; and its glorious fruits have established its character. If Abolitionists are sincere in desiring the removal of slavery from our country, and for the happiness of slaves, let them meet us on this common ground; and we will give them the right hand of fellowship.

3. Let us *pray.* "The Lord reigneth." He can remove slavery and every other evil from the country. His grace and His Providence only can do it. He works in answer to prayer. Let us give up bitter denunciation, and meet, as the children of our Heavenly Father, at the throne of grace. May God, in his mercy, give us back those halcyon days, when the whole Church of Christ, and the whole country, North and South, stood side by side in the earnest effort to remove this giant evil from the land. May he subdue evil passions, cause his watchmen to see eye to eye, bring back his Church to the unerring teachings of his Word; and then the Gospel, in its purity and power, will make this great nation the happiest nation on the globe, and a blessing to all other nations.

www.ingramcontent.com/pod-product-compliance
Lightning Source LLC
Chambersburg PA
CBHW021427090426
42742CB00009B/1288